A Dent to My Identity

Orange Books Publication

1st Floor, Rajhans Arcade, Mall Road, Kohka, Bhilai, Chhattisgarh 490020

Website: **www.orangebooks.in**

© Copyright, 2024, Author

All rights reserved. No part of this book may be reproduced, stored in a retrieval system, or transmitted, in any form by any means, electronic, mechanical, magnetic, optical, chemical, manual, photocopying, recording or otherwise, without the prior written consent of its writer.

First Edition, 2024

ISBN: 978-93-6554-476-3

A DENT TO MY IDENTITY

EXPERIENCE THE LONE BATTLE OF ARJUN

K. SATHISH KUMAR

Orange Books Publication
www.orangebooks.in

Following his emotional breakup, Arjun enters the race for leadership. Will he finally succeed in retrieving the two most crucial aspects of his life? One his identity and other being the love of his life.

Dedicated to

My Father

Mr. K.Dhana Raju, who has loved me the most in my life but to whom I couldn't reciprocate the same love..

About The Author

To know about the author and his own journey, scan the QR code above

or

Visit: www.mrcooltothecore.blogspot.com

Contents

Chapter - 1 Living A Double Life 1

Chapter - 2 Happy New Year 15

Chapter - 3 The Big Test 26

Chapter - 4 Offline To Online 37

Chapter - 5 My Partner... My Angel 50

Chapter - 6 Still Ringing 64

Chapter - 7 Money, Gold & Stocks 79

Chapter - 8 Got Caught! 89

Chapter - 9 Kill For Kill 102

Chapter - 10 The Countdown 115

Chapter - 11 The Three Colours 128

Chapter - 12 The Final Run 133

Chapter - 1
Living A Double Life

A cab arrives outside the entrance of a girl's hostel and Nithya exits the vehicle. Opens the trunk and takes the trolley bag out. The taxi leaves from the place. It is six o'clock in the morning. She knocks on door 303 and her roommate answers. Her roommate asks her why it is so important to come at this time given, that it is only a weekend. Nithya responds that she has an important work and must leave by 10 a.m.

She tosses her trolley bag aside and falls asleep on the bed.

At 9:30 am the alarm goes off; she gets out of bed and places her feet on the floor.

In an unknown place, moving up from the floor to the bed, a guy is seen seated on his bed with his feet on the floor. A few marks of the old wounds are still visible on his back. He takes the tab beside the bed lamp and sees a message that says **"MEET ME at 7:30 PM"**.

She gets ready, comes downstairs, and takes a cab. The guy also gets ready. He packs his small bag. She gets down in front of a house. Nithya rings the doorbell.

He opens the door, descends the stairs into the basement and presses a button to raise the garage shutter. There are two bikes and two cars. He approaches one of them.

A lady approaches the girl. Nithya inquires if this is Arjun's home. The lady says yes and invites her inside. He gets into one of the cars, places his bag beside him on the seat opens the tab, keeps it in front of him and starts the vehicle.

The lady motions her to take a seat and instructs her daughter to get some water first. She inquires what has brought Nithya here. Nithya responds that she came to meet her son.

His mother replies that he is not present there. She becomes emotional and begins to cry as a because of her son's absence from home on his birthday. Her daughter tries to soothe her. She asks Nithya to wait outside for a while.

He continues to drive for the next ten minutes, stops at one location.

The daughter takes a key from the key chain holder and walks out. She invites Nithya to join her. She ascends the stairs to the first floor. Nithya follows her. He activates the tablet screen, which displays live CCTV footage of a parking lot with a few vehicles parked. He is seated in his car, very relaxed and has his gaze fixed on the tablet screen.

Nithya says, "I'm sorry, I guess I came at the wrong time," as they take the steps. "I'm not sure why your brother isn't at home. I sincerely apologize."

It's fine.

It's obvious with mother's love for his son. Today being his birthday didn't help your cause.

A buzzer sound from his wrist watch draws his attention as she unlocks the door. He takes the tab in his hand. Now seated both the women look more relaxed.

"I attended the same university as your brother. He has already completed a project along the same lines as the one I am proposing. I obtained his contact information from the Department Head. I thought it would be helpful if I could speak to him once."

"Because both his phone numbers were not reachable, I assumed he would be available at home. I saw his date of birth and thought it would be nice to meet him on this day, so I rushed from SECTOR 8 this morning but he's not here," says Nithya. Very disappointedly.

"So, do you know when he'll be back?"

"Nobody knows", his sister responds. "This is not the first time he has done something like this. He'll show up one day. That is all we can hope for."

"If you don't know when he'll arrive, how will my project progress? Please assist me in some way or the other", she requests her.

"Not now." His sister responds.

They exchange their contact numbers. "I'll contact you later," said Nithya.

"Meanwhile, it would be better if you can meet his friend, he may know a thing or two about him. He's known Arjun for a long time. Vikram is his name. I don't have his phone number, but I do know where he lives."

They both go to his friend's house. Arjun notices one white car leaving the parking lot. The moment the white car leaves the parking lot, he gets alert. He keeps both hands on the steering wheel and looks in the rear-view mirror. When the white car passes by him, he begins to follow it.

They arrive at his friend Vikram's house.

To enter the highway, both the cars turn left. Arjun's car gradually overtakes the white car. Vikram's mother informs them, that he is at his workplace and will be available at home tomorrow because it is the weekend. They take his phone number and leave the scene.

At one point, both cars get parked side by side, so that they face each other from their driver's seats. Both windows are lowered. They exchange envelopes.

The windows are closed and they move away from that location.

She drops Nithya at the crossroads. Nithya takes a cab, while Arjun's sister departs for work.

Both Arjun and Nithya return to their respective rooms and collapse on their beds to take a nap. The time is 06:30 p.m. The sky is gradually getting dark. He takes his hoodie, walks out of the room to go for a jog. He moves slowly out of the neighbourhood and into the dark woods.

He crosses the main junction and walks towards the beach. After a while, he could see a large guest house at a distance. He walks slowly towards the house.

A person is seen sitting on a chair in front of a campfire. Arjun approaches him. The man rises from his seat and starts to walk towards Arjun with a smile on his face. He is a 50- year-old man who greets Arjun with a tight hug and wishes him a happy birthday.

He continues to say, "Happy birthday, Prince," several times.

Happy Birthday Arjun. My boy.

Arjun doesn't react much to his gesture. He only smiles back. They both walk towards the campfire, where a cake is waiting for him on the bench. Looking at the cake, Arjun expresses his displeasure and says, "Guruji, you know that I don't like all these things."

Nothing will happen for one day, he claims. I made it all by myself for you. I've been in the guest house since the morning. After the formalities they both settle into their respective chairs. He asks Arjun if there have been any recent developments that he should be aware of. Arjun responds with a, "No."

"Did you at least try to call home?"

Arjun shakes his head...

"You should have."

"What have you done since morning?"

Arjun replies, "Nothing much."

"What about your meal?" Arjun promises to have something in his room. Guruji claims to have prepared dinner as well. Arjun questions him on why he is doing all this.

He responds by saying that he has made Arjun's life difficult on numerous occasions. "Let me at least do something that will make you happy on your birthday Arjun," said Guruji.

"Doing things like this makes me feel redeemed."

They both stand up and proceed to the house. They both take their seats at the dining table. All the dishes are already placed on the table.

Arjun is served from the dishes. The old man goes on to say, "You should have called home. At least, your parents would be pleased and be happy."

"I'll try to contact them after the big event. Also, what do you want me to tell them if they ask about my job."

"Understood!"

Meanwhile the old man finishes his drink.

"What about the girl? What happened to her?"

Arjun becomes enraged. "I'm not thinking about her. Talking about her is pointless. Many other important things are there to pay attention to. I'd like to focus on them first."

"Anyway, why do you bother asking me again, when you already know everything?"

"Everything, you mean everything. Do you still believe that I know everything?"

Arjun doesn't respond much.

He in turn criticizes Arjun, saying that, "They both would not have been caught in this situation, if he had simply followed my orders.'

"Not right now!" Says Arjun.

"Let's stay in the present sir."

Arjun asks him, "You have a big test in the form of an interview. When will it be?"

"We are planning it for the New Year. We need to inform the public about our plans for the coming year."

Both of them finish their meal. Arjun leads him to his room. He keeps saying that, "You are my prince. I want you to succeed and make it big Arjun. You should."

Arjun confidently says that he will and gently places him on his bed. He pulls the bed sheet over him and turns on the air conditioner. He informs him that he will leave then he turns off the light and closes the door.

He shuts the primary back door, walks through the campfire. He gets to the fence. The gate is opened. Passes through it. Wears his hoody and begins to walk towards the beach he stands there for a while staring at the waves.

He pulls a photograph from his pocket. A family of four. He considers it for a moment Then looks out at the sea.

I was born on the last Friday of a decade. My mother used to say that the only thing that happened to me peacefully was my birth. After that, whether it was fate or the choices I made, nothing ever w went smoothly again. This decade still has one year left - 365 days. Whatever I've been doing for the past eight years, living a double life. Everything has to come to an end sooner or later. I am prepared for my final adventure.

The most difficult test of my life. My last best shot at success in life.

"My journey to reveal my true identity."

He keeps the photo back into his pocket. He starts walking back the same way he came. He enters his room and promptly falls asleep. Turns off the lights.

The next day Arjun sits in his cabin in front of the system. He is looking at some of the photos of the girl, that were taken at the house yesterday. Arjun sends a few photos of the girl to one of his deputies. Tells him to run a background check on that girl.

The officer takes the orders.

Arjun is seen on the computer screen attempting to solve some puzzles.

After a while Arjun gives the current location of Nithya to to another officer. Arjun directs him to follow her and keep him updated on her whereabouts. He tells him to leave right then.

The officer reaches the location. He discovers that she is alone in a coffee shop on the beach side. Arjun receives the same information from him. Arjun is now seen on the floor doing few push-ups. He tells the officer to send him one photograph of hers.

The officer agrees. After about ten minutes, the officer notices a guy approaching her table. He comes to a halt at her table and shakes hands with her. They are now seated. The officer continues to watch them.

He takes another photo of them and sends it to Arjun. Arjun recognizes the visitor as Vikram, his friend. He instructs the officer to keep an eye on them.

Vikram tells her that, "Arjun had gone to SECTOR 8 because he couldn't handle the pressure at home. He has to find some work. He felt that if he stayed there, he would be forced to work, while Annanya is yet to finish her course."

"Arjun has no idea what Annanya would plan to do after college. What if she moved out of this sector either for a job or for higher studies? What if she gets married immediately?"

"These were the thoughts racing through his mind." Vikram concludes.

Nithya suggests that, "He could have taken a job here and that if she moves out of town, he can do the same."

Vikram responds that, "It's not as simple as you think. Arjun falling in love with a girl is a huge thing to happen. Once-in-a-lifetime event. Another huge task is to get married to her."

"It's especially very difficult for an outsider to break into a well-established family and community. What will he do if she does not fall in love with him?"

"He'll end up like any other love failure guy."

"You women can always surprise us."

"Arjun, I believe is not that kind. If he wants something to happen, he will find a way or two to succeed."

"He always emphasized Annanya as his top priority in life. Other things including work can wait."

"So, did he make it?" Nithya asks.

Vikram is very clear that he never fully understands what is going on, in this man's life. They order something to eat in between. The officer in the car continues to keep an eye on them.

Vikram asks her why she wishes to meet him. She replies that she wants to do something related to the topic of marriage for her Ph.D. and her guide suggested Arjun's name because he had already collected some data on similar topic.

Vikram laughs out loudly in response.

"So, you're also interested in the topic of marriage."

She responds that her family is currently looking for a match for her, so she believes it is a good subject to work on, given her current situation.

Vikram asks her, "Are you also obsessed the same way like Arjun with marriage. You're referring to the marriage project. Arjun took me to a few places after I returned from work in the evenings?"

"I'm curious about this guy," says Nithya. "After hearing about him from his sister and now from you."

"Did he finally succeed?"

"He came to the city few months ago. Met me once, since then there has been no word from him. I asked him the same question."

His response was less than satisfactory.

Vikram thinks it's getting late. "Sorry for the late arrival today. Traffic!" he said.

"Can we meet some other day if you prefer?"

"What can we do if we happen to meet again? Asked Nithya. "I'm not sure where he is," Nithya added.

"Yes, but I know where Annanya stays. It's best if you ask her," suggested Vikram.

"That's a good thought." She replies as she gets excited.

They part ways after the bill has been paid. Arjun is informed of this. He tells the officer to stay with the girl. The officer arrives at the hostel and informs Arjun of the location. Arjun instructs him to keep an eye on her for the night and to leave in the morning when the reliever arrives.

On Monday afternoon, Nithya is seen at her office desk waiting for 4 p.m. She leaves the office goes to meet the Head of the Department at the college.

She tells her what all had happened up to this point.

The head tell her that getting in touch with this guy is difficult. He doesn't respond much. That has happened to me too. He used to just meet me in person most of the time.

The madam instructs her to choose the topic at her leisure and advises her to relax and take a break.

She said, "As your parents are also looking for matches for you, take things slowly. There's no need to come and meet me on a regular basis. When you're finished with the abstract simply email me a copy of the draft. That will be all."

She expresses her desire to know more about this guy.

The department head hands over the key of the cupboard containing their batch records. "I remember administering a few tests to him; he was far too gifted to be ordinary."

"Don't think too much about him. Just take a break."

"Wishes for the New Year in advance."

She leaves that place wishing the same to the head.

The officer is waiting outside, as she exits the building. He informs Arjun that she has come out and is on a phone call with someone. The officer inquires whether Arjun wishes to track her phone calls.

Arjun says 'NO'. "Simply observe."

"Do you know how intelligent your brother is?" Nithya asks his sister.

"He is a good student." Arjun's sister replies.

"His test results are even more intriguing. Those outcomes are remarkable. Did your brother inform you of this?"

Arjun's sister responds saying that, "He conceals a lot of things. It's not surprising that he didn't tell me."

"What about the good things?"

"Good! Bad! Hasn't shared much. So, we got used to it all. Everyone knows he is intelligent, but no one knows why he couldn't find work."

She hangs up the phone, stunned. It's 5:30 p.m. She gets on her scooter and returns to the hostel.

Arjun seated in his cabin asks the current location of the day shift officer. He instructs to ping him, once his shift is complete.

Arjun calls another person. He sends the girl's information. He instructs to conduct a family background check. Call logs from the day before yesterday to the last two-three months. Places visited. "Let me know if you notice anything suspicious." He instructed.

"Keep this as very confidential," he says at the end of the call.

He returns to his room. The officer shift is over. He calls Arjun to see, if someone can take over. Arjun tells him that there is no need to work for the night shift. He can return to her hostel, the next morning.

The officer wishes him in advance a Happy New Year. Arjun also greets him and then hangs up the phone.

Arjun finishes his dinner and goes to bed by 8:30 p.m.

After few hours, unable to sleep, he gets up and begins to drive in the middle of the night. He comes to a halt near a bar. Looks around the store. Calls one guy standing outside the bar.

He tells him to get a bottle of liquor. Gives him his card. After a few minutes the guy comes back with the bottle and returns the card. He starts the engine again and arrives at the girls' hostel.

As the girls are already immersed in the new year's party, the park adjacent to the hostel is fully illuminated. He gets stationed inside the car and watches everyone. Takes a look at the bottle.

His parents are both alone in their home.

The music becomes louder as time passes. It's 12 a.m. Everyone is celebrating and wishing each other as well. Behind the wheel, he has his family photo in front of him.

He feels sorry for his family.

Looks at the girls who are having fun; he starts his car and drives away.

Chapter - 2
Happy New Year

THE BIG DAY....

Just before the interview, the 50-year-old man receives a call from Arjun. He inquires, from the CEO if everything is in order.

"Yes," he says. "Watching the telecast?"

Definitely sir, I'm waiting for you. Best wishes, Guruji.

On the occasion of the New Year, the interviewer greets the CEO Mr. Acharya Aravind Krishna. He too greets her.

"I believe there have been some recent developments regarding the appointment of your successor sir. Is that true?

Mr. Aravind replies by saying that, "Yes the initial or first stage of selection will be held on the 10th of this month and the results will be announced on the same day."

"We heard a rumour that you had no intention of holding a competition until a few months ago and that you simply wanted to appoint someone?"

"Is this true sir?"

"Yes!"

"So why is it being done now?" The lady asks.

The CEO responds saying "May be like you, the investors, the board of directors and my family members all failed to grasp the idea behind my processes."

"That disappointed me greatly."

Arjun in his room watches the interview.

"So, the people you mentioned above are aware of all these advancements?"

"No, I was about to announce it but due to some unexpected and unavoidable circumstances, we are discussing it today."

"I received harsh criticism from all sides for not taking their advice. They were disappointed that they were not consulted or involved in the process. They began to spread false propaganda claiming that I was not concerned about the welfare of the employees or their families."

"Their actions bothered me."

"My family members began to argue about how someone other than my son, could take my place?"

"That's exactly what I was thinking. You chose someone other than your son to be your successor?"

"What compelled you to proceed?"

"It's difficult to explain everything right now. People here are aware of the circumstances surrounding my appointment to this position.

My recent actions were not well received by my family members. They were concerned that the family inheritance would be lost. I know what we all went through before the separation, decades ago. I know what my grandfather went through to establish this company, as well as what my father did later."

"Is your son aware of all this?"

"As I previously stated, let us not go to the past."

"Sir, I understand your concern. A lot of emotions are at stake. Let us take a quick break."

During the break, Arjun over a phone call, - "Masterji in nice flow ah! Given the pace the interview may end sooner than expected."

Back to the interview…

"So, how did you have this competition?"

"The Board of Directors and other family members made the decision. Each board of directors nominate one individual from their side. The majority of them are members of my family. The participating candidate would be chosen by them."

"I will design the process of selecting the final one. That's how everyone got on the same page."

"So, I guess we'll have ten contestants. There are nine board members and one candidate from your side. Is that right, sir?"

"No."

"There will be 12 contestants. Other than the 9, one from the secret service division. They are usually not present at Board of Directors meetings because it is a separate division. This time, however they are also involved. My son and the candidate I've already chosen."

"Oh, your son is also taking part? I thought he wasn't going to be available."

"He certainly will!"

"So, we finally have 12 participants rearing to go on the 10th of this month."

"So, Sir can we know who the contestants will be?"

"Obviously, the answer would be NO."

"All the information regarding how the competition is designed, the voting process and who is involved will be provided in due course of time."

"Sir, before we conclude the interview, do you have anything to say to the employees of the organization and other fraternities?"

"I just want to say that whatever decisions I have taken previously, I have been honest with integrity and keeping in mind the best interests of all the members of this organization and the people of this state. On this New Year's Eve, I'd like to wish everyone a prosperous New Year. For the next 365 days, let's try to create a new family, beyond blood relations and I hope you'll all join me in this initiative. This year is dedicated to you."

"We are ensuring that everyone is involved in this process including stakeholders, employees and their families. We will provide all relevant information in the coming days."

"So, sir, I hope everything goes as planned and we will be led by the right person in the near future."

"Yeah. Thank you all."

The interview comes to an end.

It's noon and Vijay abruptly awakens from a dream and knocking the bed lamp onto the floor. His wife storms out from the kitchen and into the bedroom, yelling at him. "That is why I advised you not to go again for field jobs."

"Everything would have been so beautiful if I had listened to my father. There is no peace. For the rest of my life, I will live in the same company quarters and die here too. When are we going to move into a new apartment? Even New Year's day is a normal day for me."

"If you go to office now, when are you going to come back?"

He advises her not to start the day with such squabbles.

She looks at him as she stands next to the door. "Was that the same bomb blast in the dream?" He gets out of the bed. Requests for a cup of coffee from her.

He gets ready and drives away. His boss calls to inquire about his whereabouts. He replies he is on the way to the office.

Vikram drives Nithya to Annanya's house. The officer updates Arjun. He leaves after showing her the building. She pays Annanya a visit and explains why she's there.

She asks Annanya when she first met him. Annanya told her that she can't go all over telling her about him. As she is slowly getting over it now."

"Okay, when was the last time you saw him?" She responds with a NO.

Nithya looks disappointed, as she has no idea what to do next. Annanya inquires as to why he is of interest to her. With his kind of grades, he should have had no trouble finding work. "He did not take a job because you were still studying and he does not know what your next step in life will be. As the pressure grew at home, he left this sector for you." Nithya told Annanya.

"You are the most important person of his life. Who does these things for a woman?"

Annanya is unaware that he is avoiding work because of her.

"Why should he do all these things, I envy you."

"Enough praising him."

"He used to send digital postcards. I left them at my uncle's house."

"If you want, I can get them back for you. That is all I can do for you at this time."

"Can I have your phone number?"

No phone numbers. Come back after a week.

She starts to leave the room. When she gets to the door, she asks, "When did he send those cards?"

She replies that it was during her final year of MBA.

"So, you were here only at that time?" She replies with a simple, "Yes."

She asks her, "Why are the cards at your uncle's house implying that you took them along with you when you left this place."

"So, you were interested. You like him." Nithya says with a smile on her face.

Annanya hurls a pillow at her. Nithya shuts the door and comes out.

She returns to her scooter with a smile on her face. Starts from there and returns to the hostel. The officer updates the same to Arjun. Arjun tells him to stick around.

FEW YEARS BACK…

A group of people are seated across a round table, with a small ray of light projecting on the table from the top and darkness surrounding them. An individual begins to speak. Let me explain her daily schedule.

"The car travels from home to college with two other cars, one in front and one behind. The cars enter the campus and come to a halt in front of her department."

"Vijay exits the first car and opens the back door of the second car for Meghna to get down. Her friends are

expecting her. The security guard from the third car also gets out and follows her into the building."

Arjun in his green checked shirt and blue jeans is seen coming in the opposite direction as she enters the building. She smiles and wishes him.

Arjun reciprocates.

She takes the steps, as he exits the building.

Arjun walks through the parking lot, past the vehicles, and into the library on the other side.

"Her class room is on the third floor, sir. She spends the majority of her time inside the building for classes. A couple of security guards are at the building's entrance and another couple on the third floor."

"Both the drivers and Vijay are standing in the parking lot, watching the girl who is sitting near the classroom window."

Arjun is seated across on another table in the library. Opens his laptop. In addition to the existing one camera is attached to the sunshade of the library building and is aimed directly at the girl. Arjun uses his laptop to view the footage of the girl sitting in the classroom.

"Vijay is also watching the footage on his tablet inside his car."

"She doesn't come out every day during lunch. The classes would get over at 4:00 p.m. At times, by the end of the day she would leave immediately in her cars or hang out with her friends in the college for a while sir."

"She usually gets back around 5:30 p.m. Evening schedules are not always consistent. They may or may not come out. Obtaining their itinerary is difficult."

"The cars are at the house from night to morning, and guards are stationed all around the house, sir."

Another voice interrupts- "Did I hire you to hear all this useless information. Look for a specific time to carry out our plan and let me know, how you intend to do so in a week."

The team responds with a resounding "YES." Then the light goes out.

BACK TO PRESENT…

Arjun dials his sister's number, using his satellite phone. She inquiries about his whereabouts.

"I'm fine," he says.

She asks him, "Whose number is this?"

He tells her that it's his friend's number.

She inquires whether he is preparing for any competitive exams. She continues to question him about why he didn't call on his birthday. "Mom had been waiting for your call all day. She was in tears," she says.

Arjun replies, "Tell her to be patient for a little longer."

"You also did not call for the New Year. You are not concerned about your family. You are not concerned about what may happen to us, "she continued.

"Not like that, you know what I'm like," says Arjun.

"Do you really think about us anymore?"

"I am always there for you. I realize this is my last chance. I promise you my return will be spectacular. I can guarantee it."

"At the very least, try to find some work," she concludes.

"Hmm ok."

"Any other news to share?"

She tells him about the girl who had come to meet him. He takes her number and immediately hangs up the phone.

Nithya receives a phone call from Arjun. She inquires about when she can meet with him. She explains why.

He answers with a, "No."

She then says, "It's fine because I have other people to meet with."

"So, who else did you run into?"

"Your bestie and your …. love."

"She's not my love" …

"So, what happened after that?"

"Why do you want to know everything?"

"Curiosity" …

"Your friend is unaware of what is going on at home. She has no idea what your friend knows. The family is unaware of her. It's very intriguing."

"You're pushing the boundaries?" Arjun says.

"There isn't much to say about me."

"No, I don't believe so." Nithya stresses.

"Fine. What exactly do you want?"

"I need your assistance with the project."

"I can assist you, but only under one condition."

"What exactly is it?"

"I don't want you meet her again. I don't want you to disturb her."

"It will be difficult, but I will try. Partially acceptable."

"I have a question for you?" Nithya says.

"If she dislikes you. Why did she take those cards with her?"

Arjun reiterates with another question.

"If she really liked me? Why didn't she bring them back?"

He hangs up the phone.

Chapter - 3
The Big Test

Day 1

Contestants are numbered from C1 to C12. Arjun's number is C7. All the participants are made to assemble in the facility by 4pm. Each one is given a separate room as accommodation.

At 6pm they will be administered with a personality assessment test named TAT. Assessment will be done simultaneously by the seasoned professionals.

No elimination on Day 1- it's just for personality assessment. After the assessment, report will be prepared on each and every individual and the same will be published online immediately.

Day 2: 10 AM

The entire process is broadcasted live to the public. The competition will be divided into three stages. Scores will be displayed on the leader board. Their vitals will be monitored, throughout the exam and presented on the large screen along with their scores.

Stage 1: The time duration is 2 hours with four sets of 30 minutes each.

The first set has 100 questions. As the sets progresses, the number of questions would reduce to 75, 50, and 25. As the set number increases so would the difficulty level. In addition, the score for each correct answer will also increase.

Each set of questions would cover the following topics: The establishment of this organization and its presence in all industries. The corporation is involved in a number of industries. Analytical reasoning and logical thinking are also tested. English as well as business administration.

At the start of each set, all the questions for the contestants to answer, will be displayed. It is their choice to answer any question in the lot but the catch is that, if a contestant answers that question correctly, the score goes to that individual and the remaining contestants cannot answer that question. The question will freeze. Contestants can see how many questions have been answered, as well as how many remain unanswered.

Each contestant can answer each question only once. And the incorrect answers will result in a negative score. On their monitors only the individual score will be displayed. Every fifteen minutes the scores of all the twelve contestants, will be displayed on their screens.

Viewers watching the live broadcast will get to know the scores of the participants all along the competition. All individual scores will be shown on the leader board at the end of stage 1. The top ten will advance to the next round.

Arjun finishes third after stage 1.

Stage 2 begins after lunch.

STAGE 2: It's time to put their physical abilities to the test.

This stage includes four activities.

Activity 1: MMA (five rounds)

Each round will last for five minutes, with a 30 second break period in between.

They are challenged by professionals and this activity is not carried out among the competitors.

Archery is the second activity.

In each round, each archer will have two minutes to shoot three arrows. The cycle repeats three times.

Activity 3: Paintball (2 rounds of 30 minutes each). This is conducted among the contestants.

Activity 4: Sports Climbing- Three set of walls

Scores for each round and level would be immediately updated for public viewing.

Arjun wins round 2, but is closely followed by two other contestants. After the round 2 the total number of candidates has now been reduced to eight.

One hour break after the completion of this stage.

STAGE 3: Back to the monitors.

4 puzzles games are considered for this stage.

Suduko-3 games

Chess – 4 games

Crossword puzzles-3 games

Maze-4 games

Each contestant will play a total of 14 games and will face each other twice.

Overall scores are added up after the completion of three stages and five candidates make the final cut.

Arjun makes the final cut.

Next step will be updated to the public after two days break. The losers will return home while the 5 winners will stay in the facility provided until further instructions are given.

AT THE TABLE- group of people discussing.

"So, when is the date?"

A project expo will be conducted on the 10th of this month, which provides a better opportunity to abduct the girl. All the models will be displayed in the basement of a building.

One person will be at the juice stall. The other two will take their positions inside. The lady finishes off by saying that she will enter the college through the cab that is scheduled and will get her part done.

Okay fine. This time around I don't want any last-minute complications.

We made all the necessary arrangements to execute our plan sir. This time for sure we will succeed sir.

Each of the final contenders is moved to a different floor of a huge facility with high levels of security. Each of them is given a significant number of employees consisting of spokespersons, coordinators and experts from various businesses. They also have an assistant who helps to plan everything and serves as a communication link between the contestants and their team members.

Arjun is seated in his cabin, which is similar to the one, he has previously used. He looks out through the huge opaque glass window. Everyone on the team starts to settle down. Each and every department is segregated. The entire hall plan is presented to Arjun.

The day before the exhibition:

In the canteen Arjun and his friends are having lunch. One of his friends shows him an advertisement for a car company which states that if we purchase the car, they would offer free movie tickets every Friday and one free water service every month at the designated malls, where the owner goes to watch the movie. This offer can be availed, if purchased during this festive season.

They joke around saying that if they had that much money, they would go to the movies for the rest of their lives rather purchasing a car.

Arjun's team inspects the location separately rather along with Vijay's team and they provide assurance for her visit. After having his lunch Arjun alone inspects the location.

Its 6 p.m.

Arjun returns to the exhibition hall to meet Vikram. Vikram is a member of the student club that is organizing the expo. He is taking care of the arrangements there.

Arjun inquiries about his whereabouts. Vikram responds that majority of the work has been completed.

Arjun looks around. They leave the place at 6:30 p.m.

Arjun addresses the spokesperson and in charges from each industry.

"We have a huge task in front of us. Do you have any ideas where to begin?"

One of them says, "Sir, which industry shall we start?"

Arjun says, "There is no particular industry, but let's start with every sector and industry, wherever we have our footprints. I require a detailed organizational structure of all the departments in those industries. Number of job positions involved, their job descriptions and also their salary packages."

"Whether it is an industry or service, I want the work structure of each and every department."

"I need all of the information within one week!"

"How is it possible in one week sir?"

"Start the work and I will assist you." He speaks.

Arjun instructs the coordinators of each division to keep him updated about the duties allocated to all their team members.

"I want all the spokesperson and the coordinators to work in tandem."

"Meghna and her friends walk out of their building." Vijay and his team accompany them. Arjun's team is also with them. They stop at the juice stall before heading to the exhibition. They order a beverage.

The lady enters into the college in the cab. The car stops near one substation. She gets down the car. She meets the chief engineer there. They continue to have a conversation.

Before offering her the juice, he mixes something. Meghna drinks the juice. The manager shows the panel in which one breaker, has to be placed. She asks them whether the back-up power is working or not before turning off the supply.

The manager replies that the backup is in place. She checks her watch once.

The girls finish their drink and they move to the other stalls. Meanwhile the guy at the juice stall, double checks his watch. He presses one button in his watch and the display shows number 10. He leaves the stall and begins to walk towards the big building.

"Where is my secretary?" Asks Arjun through his mouthpiece.

The secretary responds, "Sir!"

"Location wise I'd like to know what ingredients we are rich in. Every location has some significance or is famous for something. Gather those details as soon as possible. Assign the task to the survey and the data team."

"I'd want to see a map of our state on the big screen behind me."

"Highlight each of the 12 sectors as well as their zones and consequently their divisions on the big screen. I need all of these details on my table by the end of the day."

"I want the details of the people, who are registered with our company. Employees and non-employees. Everyone who is availing our services."

"EVERYONE WHO IS PROBABLY GOING TO VOTE"

The lady forgets to give the gift from the company to the manager - a digital wall clock. She gets back to the desk, opens her bag and offers him the gift. She requests him to open and check whether it's working properly or not. She further suggests him to hang it onto his wall behind his desk as it's a nice place for the clock to settle in. He obliges.

They once again move to the panel.

Near the south of the building a catering vehicle is stationed outside the bank. Vessels containing the dishes are being taken inside. The guy from the juice stall approaches the vehicle. He talks to the workers and later gets into the driver's seat. The unloading is completed. He orders the workers to go inside the bank to serve the dishes.

He later takes the permission from the bank's security guard to park the vehicle behind the big building as its shady there. He gets down the catering vehicle. Goes to open the lock of back side entrance, which hasn't been used for months. Gets back into the car. Seated. Once again presses the button. This time the number is 8. He seems relaxed and keeps an eye on his watch.

Arjun is nowhere seen around all this time.

The lady opens the panel door. The lady continues to work near the panel doing some testing. Quietly she also presses the button and number 7 displays on the screen.

The same number is displayed on the drivers watch also. He has a smile on his face.

The girls now start moving towards the big building. Vijay and his men accompany them. Arjun's team too comes forward.

Arjun yet to receive the information he asked for, speaks to his secretary. He orders her not to think much at this stage and provide him the data that he requires.

She complies.

He tells her to convey the same to everyone. "They will get their chance to speak or ask queries but not right now. I believe that for the last five years consolidated data on people's income and segregation based on various income slabs and other earnings has been done. I need those details." Arjun said.

"Get all the details from the concerned departments.

Youth (studying, unemployed and employed) those details also. Present passed out students count."

"How many positions were opened in our organization over the last two to three years?"

"I want that count. I also need that information on estimated jobs positions in near future based on current situation."

"In addition to that the number of students to graduate in the next 4-5 years. Pay scales and amounts estimated for salaries and employee welfare. I'd like to see the economics covered as well. Not exact figures, but 95% accuracy will do the job at this stage." He briefed.

The secretary has a puzzled look on her face. Arjun watches her from his monitor and continues to say. "Don't give me that kind of look." She gets alert.

"Don't Worry I will keep a mail stating the documents required."

"Ok sir."

She appears relaxed now.

The girls enter the exhibition area. The fest is conducted in the basement of the building. Arjun comes into live. He gives instructions to his team members. He informs them that it's time to split up. Vijay disagrees but Arjun continues to give instructions.

He orders Vijay and his team to stay with the girls, while his team would split up. He tells one of the team members to go out of the building and stay at the north east corner point of the building. The other member is instructed to stay at the open parking place, where a few vehicles are parked. The parking place is in the south of the building. She obliges. To the third officer, he instructs him to go to the first floor and look for the stairs at the back side of the building and tells him to stay there until instructed.

One of the officers asks Arjun, where actually he is. Arjun says that he is doing his job, tells him to do the same.

"Don't Worry Guys."

"Always there for you. Want you to stay focused."

"What courses are offered at each college? Cover each and every sector. Overall, at what all places these courses are offered. The annual number of seats available at the college. If a technological or practical application is required for that course, how close is the institution to that industry? Note that." He said.

"Are there any other courses available at other institutions but not at ours? Is there anything unique about those courses? Are there any plans to build new colleges? How close do they intend to build these institutions to industries? I want all those future proposals and projects list." Demanded arjun.

"I need the number of faculties present and the assessment reports of other faculty members... I want one web page created for each information that I'm asking for. Send me the details ASAP."

"I WANT EVERYTHING TO BE ORGANISED AS MUCH AS POSSIBLE."

Chapter - 4
Offline To Online

The exhibition area is fully crowded. A man with a mask from the first aid team moves towards the girls. He took an injector from his pocket and shoots it into her feet. After that he also presses the button in the watch. The countdown continues and this time 5 is displayed. 10 seconds after that the lady removes the breaker. She presses the button again. Number 3 is displayed. As the power gets turned off in the exhibition hall, Meghna starts fainting.

With just a faint light in the exhibition hall, the masked man attacks the guards and takes them down quickly. People in the exhibition area start to run in all direction out of fear, while Meghna is taken by the other guy. He tries to escape by cutting one flexi, which is covering the way to the backstairs of the building. He also presses the button in his watch, number 2 gets displayed.

Arjun is informed about the current situation, he tells both the officers, who are outside the building to move towards the west side of the building. As soon as the kidnapper tries to go towards the opened gate, he is mildly injured by the bullet pain simulator, which is shot by the officer, who has been waiting at the stairs. The injury makes him drop the girl, whom he is carrying on his shoulder. Meghna falls on the floor.

The officer at the stairs tells his other two team members to come to his current location. Arjun tells them not to move. Both of them get into a fight. The officer gets badly injured. The kidnapper tries to pick up the girl again.

Meanwhile Vijay reaches the place, unable to lift the girl again and seeing Vijay, the kidnapper decides to leave the place alone. He passes through the opened gate and goes near the catering vehicle, only to find out that the driver is dead.

He presses another button, which displays "MISSION ABORT". Seeing the same message, the lady has a disappointed look on her face.

"Based on the income data and how the state is divided into Sectors, Zones and Divisions (Urban Division and Rural Division) can we develop the family trees of all the resident families registered in our company? Is it possible?" Asked Arjun.

One of the spokespersons responds that it is quite difficult. Arjun gives a thought

"Okay then!"

"At least how many people are staying in each house number? Start with a street, then a division and gradually work your way up to sectors. The overall count should match our population. Can we try this approach? Is it possible for us to get this information?"

"We'll give it a shot, Sir?"

"Good."

The overhead satellite camera operator operating from a remote place informs Arjun that one vehicle is reversing behind the big building and they lost the vision, as the vehicle is under the big sunshade now. Arjun is sheltered under a tree and is already looking at the vehicle. He tells the operator not to worry.

The vehicle stops and the driver steps out of the vehicle and walks towards the gate to open it. Arjun keeps watching him from under the tree. He opens it and gets back to the vehicle.

Arjun now starts walking towards the vehicle. The driver keeps an eye on his watch. Arjun is now behind the trunk. The driver is still unaware of Arjun's presence and is still looking at the watch. Arjun quickly turns left and gets to the door, opens it and firmly twists the driver head to his side in a flash and leaves from that place.

He tells the operator that everything is fine and orders him to get back to the entrance of the building and lock it as his current viewing spot. He obliges.

Currently stuck at the catering vehicle, the kidnapper is trapped with 2 officers on either side. Arjun is updated about the situation. Arjun tells Vijay to take the girl and the officer to the hospital immediately.

The guy starts to run towards one of the officers, gets into a fight. The officer on the other side starts to run towards them. The kidnapper takes down the first officer and as soon the other officer approaches him he shoots another pain simulator bullet but misses. He tries to escape by running towards the nearby stairs and the lady goes after him.

They enter a tree plantation, with the former running towards a moving college bus among other vehicles which is about to leave the campus. Arjun is updated about the current situation by the lady behind the guy and tells him that they might lose him and asks him his current location.

Arjun replies not to worry, as they have the overhead satellite visuals. We can keep tracking his movements. The kidnapper gets into the bus, the conductor objects. He points out a gun at him. Just after passing through the gate, the bus stops. He gets down from the bus. There's a local taxi parked outside the college.

He threatens the cab driver, pulls him out of the car and starts to drive fast through the road way. As he starts to move forward, the personnel operating the overhead satellite camera updates the same to Arjun.

As the cab moves past from the college buses which are parked on the left side of the road, Arjun on his bike slowly comes out of the buses track and gets mingled with the traffic and starts following the cab.

The lady at the gate is attended by the other officer who comes in a car. She gets into the car and asks Arjun for an update. He shares his location with the officers. The officers ask Arjun whether the local police need to be informed or not, but he denies as there is a backup from the satellite guy.

After a few minutes the cab enters into a hospital parking lot. Arjun tries to enter the same parking lot but the security guy blocks him and guides him to a bifurcation leading to the two -wheeler parking because of which he misses the sight of that cab. He updates his current location to his team members who are seconds away from the hospital.

Midway through sliding into the two- wheeler parking area, he parks his bike to the side and starts running towards the four wheeler parking. While in pursuit of that parking area, he is blocked by a group of workers coming out as their shift has just ended.

Before his arrival, his team reaches the cab, seeing them he stops midway. They find that the kidnapper has escaped. Arjun is updated about the same. Arjun instructs the satellite guy to keep an eye on the exit path. After a minute, the satellite guy updates that 2 sets of three black cars have left the hospital in the opposite direction and he is confused as to follow which one.

Arjun is livid with himself. He instructs the officers to check the CCTV footage of the parking lot. Few minutes later, the officers get back to him saying that it's already kept in loop.

Arjun gets in touch with his BOSS to update the current situation. He tells his team members to get back to the hospital where Meghna is admitted. Arjun leaves the bike at the hospital and gets back to college via public transport.

He again gets a call from his boss and instructs him to meet him in the evening.

Looking at his monitor he instructs one of the spokespersons to create slabs for age groupings, family earnings and income resources. He asks them to find who is the primary breadwinner in the family? How many individuals are still studying? What is the educational background of the entire family? How many people are unemployed?

"How many people do not have a formal education? I want that information segregated." asked Arjun.

"How can I learn about every single family? Based on the area and depending on the average population in the streets they need to allot one representative to ascertain the number of families. Also, the family earnings.

"I want all the segregation shown on the map behind me. In the midst of this, a spokesperson pops up to ask a question. "Sir, what are we going to do with all this information?"

Arjun responds by saying that, "Can we develop specific job mela based on the profiles we acquired and their educational background?"

"This is only for persons in the lower half of the income spectrum. How many of them have registered to vote or are eligible to vote? Gather that information as well."

The spokespersons appear to be interested with the idea.

"Also, if more people are from less educated backgrounds, where do they come from? How long have they been like this and how can we change this in the eyes of their children? So, the number of families residing in a region as well as their family income should be genuine.

Jobs and the number of positions might not be the same but students with different qualifications can apply for it with some training, after gaining the job or learn after finishing their primary course. Consider this possibility as well. List out the positions for which they can be recruited.

Arjun tells his secretary to convey one message to all the team members that they can now post any queries to him anytime via a cc mail to secretary. After few minutes one of the employees poses a question to Arjun that where is the revenue going to come to the company as he is planning to place a lot of jobs in the coming years.

Arjun is being updated the same by the secretary. Arjun acknowledges it and directly calls that employee and speaks to him.

In the evening Arjun meets his boss at an unknown location. His boss asks," Arjun what have you done today, how could he kill someone in the college?"

"Is this your way of doing things?"

Arjun replies with a "Yes." He continues saying that the other guy is lucky, as he didn't take him down.

"These kinds of actions are not accepted Arjun."

Arjun aggressively says, "Sir you better tell me who is trying to kidnap her or this will continue? I am not going to spare anyone?"

'Your job is only to protect her?'

'For that the other team is there! Why me again?'

'I don't like someone telling me how to get my job done?'

'Have you got any clues now?' The boss asked.

Arjun's phone rings.

He takes the call and leaves from that place angrily.

Arjun arranges another meeting with all the spokesperson. He tells them, "We have already mapped the organizational structure of each and every industry. Now I want the turnovers of each one."

"I want overall turnover and individual turnover. Imports, exports, services everything. Not only ours but all our contractors. Their work orders and payments."

"I know all the data is already ready. So, I am giving only one week time for this. All categories of income (Taxes, licensing, fines/penalties, and grants). I want the real numbers. Also estimate turnover and expenditure for next three years."

"From this part I want to know how my money is flowing. Where are the big numbers? Who are associated with those big numbers? Their family trees. Also, among them how many of them will be getting registered for this voting? I need that information also."

"Is there anything I missed?"

One of the spokesperson responds by saying, "Sir, What about the borrowing, the money we had lend to other big companies," sir.

"Good one," Arjun reciprocates.

Where is the data available for all these borrowings?

"The BANKS Sir."

"Right, let us concentrate on them now. I want the flow of money from all the banks."

While leaving from the location where Arjun met his boss he continues to speak to the officer on the other side. The officer on the other side tells Arjun that they had gone to the address he gave, gathered some things from that place and are heading to the office now. Arjun tells them to look for any clues or evidence and keep him posted.

"Sir, most of the money is linked with the companies doing our projects."

"All companies (small or big- third party players) which are associated with us. I want their numbers also- depending on the enterprise (small, medium and large) and how many employees are there in each company."

"I want the number of companies in each sector, zone and divisions and their valuation list."

"I need a presentation of the following categories related to the industries."

'PRODUCTION, MANFACTURING AND PROCESSING'

"How many industries are there in each category? Which sectors are they located? Make sure that the Block chain technology is integrated into all the financial transactions."

"Concentrate on the following banking services: Foreign Trade, Rural Bank (Villages), Commercial, Cooperative, Small Scale Industries Bank."

"With respect to foreign Investment, it cannot be directly done by our contractors. That money has to come to our company account. Once after the background check of the investor is done and verified then only it will be used for spending." Arjun elaborated.

The spokesperson obliges with a smile.

At Arjun's home. He is dressed in blue checkered shirt and is ready to leave for college. His father asks him about his competitive exam.

'When is the exam?'

'In two weeks,' time'. Arjun responds.

'How is the preparation going?'

He responds he is preparing well.

'Did the hall ticket come?'

'No.'

'When will the result come?'

'May be two months after the exam.'

'Good. Prepare well for the exam.'

'Sure Dad.'

'He leaves for the college.'

While seated in the library, Arjun gets the call from his boss. Asks him how he got the location of stay of that driver.

Arjun asks him what will he do after knowing now.

'Then why didn't you inform anybody?'

'It's better, if these kinds of things happen to her at times, she will be vigilant and careful.'

'She is not serious about her career also.'

'How can you do this Arjun? Don't you have emotions?'

'I am looking for solutions sir, not emotions.'

'I have an exam in two weeks' time. I have to prepare. The girl is safe now. She will be discharged in another 24 hours. Nothing to worry much?'

'Bye sir.'

He hangs the phone.

The CEO doesn't look pleased.

'Now whatever tasks or work was shortlisted in the organization chart, how much money is required, how much is to be spent. For all these tasks how much equipment is imported and how much is self-made by the company. List them.'

'Self-made means by us and not by contractors or companies outside our state.' Arjun insists.

'As list of industries is already available with us, how much GDP are they contributing and how can we make it double in next three or four years. Estimate those things.'

'Which regions specialize in certain types of product manufacturing? I have already requested this data. Where can I find it?

Arjun continues to speak. 'I have only one MOTTO.'

"EASE OF DOING BUSINESS"

After six months of taking up his job, Arjun in his favourite blue checks shirt and black jeans speaks to his boss. He asks for a favour. He continues saying that they have to convert every transaction to online transactions or at least cashless.

This has to be implemented all over. Not just to our companies but among employees and their families.

'Is it possible?' Asks the CEO.

'I want you to talk to the council sir'.

'You want me to understand the functioning your company, this state and all the sectors but the finances are so diversified to understand. I can't keep a track of everything. I need this favour from you Sir.'

'Arjun It's still early for you. Isn't this a big call?' the CEO suggests.

'Trust me Sir.'

'I need the council's approval,' says the CEO.

'Please get it,' sir.

'I have an idea about how to put it into action,' says Arjun very confidently.

'Arjun, it will take a long time to implement it completely.'

'Let it take sir. Let us start with the first step, sir.'

'I will present you with a road map and an overall plan of action. I will certainly keep all your money safe.'

'Trust me on this sir'. Arjun keeps pleading to his boss.

'You have given me a big task Arjun.'

'Okay, let me give it a shot.'

'Give me some time to think Arjun.'

"Thank You Sir".

"Love you, Sir".

He hangs the phone.

CEO has a smile on his face.

Chapter - 5
My Partner... My Angel...

Nithya and Vikram are seated in a coffee shop. He tells her about an incident where he and Arjun went to meet a lady in a marriage bureau. Arjun considers it to be as an auspicious moment and wears a yellow solid shirt with blue jeans. The lady hands him the registration form. He tells her that his parents are in sector X and he is working as an assistant professor in this sector. Vikram is taken aback and attempts to intervene. Currently Vikram is working as an assistant professor. Arjun stops him and suggests him to be silent for a while.

He begins to fill out the form. In between he comes out of the office. He calls his masterji and explains the situation. He informs him that he has given one of his contact numbers in a marriage bureau. Mentioned his and his wife's name as his father and mother. I will give that sim to you. Thus, requests him to take care if anything comes his way.

'Yeah! Sure son.'

He hangs up the phone and walks inside. He completes filling the form. Take a picture of it with his phone and gives the form to her. The lady inquires whether he has any special requirements. 'No,' he says.

He asks her to show as many profiles as possible. 'Can you show them right now?'

The lady advises Arjun not to become too excited.

'What else do you require, madam?' He asked.

'If you want me to pay the entire fee, I will do so right now.'

The lady examines the completed paperwork.

'There is no own house. Decent salary. She continues reading the other information as well.'

'It could take some time, sir.' She replies.

'I am good at heart. What else do you require from me, ma'am?'

'You may have a good heart, but people also look for other things in marriage, sir. We must also respect their choice also.'

'Yes, ma'am, you are right'. Arjun responds with great energy. So, when am I going to see the profiles.'

'Just give me some time, I'll get back to you sir.'

'Sure Ma'am.'

Both the friends depart from that place. Nithya asks Vikram what happened after that.

'From the next year all job postings, vacancies, and information about the department allotted to people should be available on a single website. What is the percentage of candidates chosen on merit and based on family income levels? Is it possible for me to have that percentage right now?'

'We will try sir.'

'I'd like an estimate of how long it will take to select a candidate solely on merit and not on financial background.'

'So, the student's academic performance should be considered. Students' grades and observations of student behaviour will be used as a criterion.'

'Continuous monitoring is required. Attach reports from class instructors and counsellors.'

'How many high-level jobs are available for our brightest and smartest students? I don't want them to leave the company. How can we encourage them to join our organization?'

Doubt from one of the members as he gets the opportunity to pose a question during the discussion.

'What if, despite numerous trials an individual is not selected? How will the family run?'

'One thing we can do is, based on the information from his profile and his abilities we can train him in a suitable course for which, we should be aware of his interests and capabilities.'

Seated in his car Arjun watches the footage of the event. After a while he gets a call from one of the officers stating that they gathered some information about the driver from his roommate.

'He is a nobody sir. The roommate gave him shelter. He was a friend during school days. Dropped from nowhere. He has been doing some odd jobs off late.'

'Run his facial id in our database?' 'What are the other officers doing?'

'All are here only sir. Three guys interrogating one fellow!'

'I am sending a photo of a student. Find him. Another person needs to find out the reason why there was a power-cut? How come we don't know about the catering vehicle? Vehicle parking is not allowed at that place? How come it's there at that time?'

'I want answers guys.'

'Sure Sir.'

'His belonging and other things which were collected yesterday are at the office Sir. It will be good if you can take a look.'

'Sure, I will.'

'Get back to your work.'

Information regarding debts and money lent to various companies is presented to Arjun. He takes a look at the numbers.

He asks the concerned department, 'How fast is the money paid back? What did they keep for security? I need those details.'

'I need valuation reports of those assets. How much are we on the safe side?'

One of the Spokesperson reminds the event of merger of the banks.

12 banks merged into 6 banks of all sectors.

Arjun also recollects that moment.

On the occasion of New Year, Arjun in his favourite black solid shirt and blue denims calls to his boss.

'I need a New Year gift from you Sir.'

'What is it Arjun?'

'How many banks do we have?'

'10'

'I want them to be reduced to 6.'

'Why?'

'There are few weaker banks. Running them individually doesn't have any returns to us.'

'Plus, the existing number is too much to keep an eye on the operation of these banks..

'I found some irregularities. If you want, I can explain in detail later.'

'Ok let's meet in the evening.'

'As we know that banks are merged from 10 to (6+1) depending on specific areas, those banks are specialized ranging from industries to rural agricultural banks. I guess the merger is done for the good.'

'What's your take on all this?' Arjun asks the spokesperson.

'Not all the spokespersons' views are on the same page on this'

'Arjun continues his briefing. An individual can have accounts opened in any of the 4 banks. Keep a limit on that.'

'Another aspect is the Stock market. I want to know about the investment by public in Stocks. All these details are to be linked to their profile via their SSN.'

'How many people are saving or investing in our banks and how are we investing that money back in the market? How much is the public risking and how much are we risking?'

One fine day Arjun calls to his boss.

'Guruji I saw her.'

'Who?'

'Finally!'

'Who? What are you talking about Arjun?'

'Did u get any clue?'

'I saw my girl sir.'

'In the college! Could you believe that?' Arjun continues with excitement.

'We both are in the same college. Such a great feeling. She will be around me.'

'My Angel who came to this college, only for me.'

'Angel beauty in my favourite black dress.'

'I'm also in my solid black shirt. What a coincidence sir ji.'

'She is my girl. That is fixed. Marriage is the only thing left.'

'Arjun Arjun' ... CEO tries to interrupt Arjun.

'What did I tell you before taking up this job?'

'I forgot everything. Have you said anything?'

He chuckles.

'Arjun!'

'No girlfriends. No relationships.'

'Yess Yes'...

'No girlfriends. No relationships.'

'But who said she is my girlfriend. She is my wife Sir. My Partner. My Angel.'

CEO tries to apply some brakes. Arjun did not like that, 'let me say something.'

'I am in a great mood and joy sir. Do not disrupt it sir.'

'Bye Sir. Call you later.'

'Arjun - Arjun.' The CEO has a helpless look on his face.

They find out the student. The footage is shown to him. Asked him about a particular individual. The student said that he couldn't get any sponsorship for his project and one week before the event he got call from the institute that one party was interested. They already saw his demo and are willing to sponsor. Their representative will come directly on that day itself. They have done the payment to the institute.

'Which Institute?'

The student gives the name of the institute.

All the vehicles numbers that entered the college during the event were also checked. Also, last minute gate passes were issued. That list also has been taken. At the substation the officers enquire. 'Why there was a power cut at that time and also what happened to the backup power?'

The manager replies that, 'As this is a new substation one switch has to be installed. The day before after we left the office, a mail had come that an engineer is going to visit the substation. I checked the mail only in the morning. They told to arrange the gate pass and also the return vehicle which I had arranged sir.'

'She came and went on to get her job done. Some paper works and she left from this place sir. One of our vehicles was leaving to town. She left in that vehicle.'

Arjun is listening to the whole conversation over his ear piece. 'What about the backup power, was there a delay, ask him,' says Arjun.

'The back-up generator was fine until that point sir, our boys checked it a day before also but don't know why it didn't turn ON at that moment.'

'What about CC footage?'

As it is a new substation cameras are yet to be installed. Arjun tells the officers to check the vehicle by which she came and also where she was dropped.

Arjun continues to discuss with one team and their spokesperson regarding family finances. They try to consider how a family is trying to cope with their financial situation.

'We need to know about their expenditures and savings (other than regular expenditures and health expenditures) so that we may determine, whether we should provide any free health care facilities for them in order to reduce their expenditure. I think our bank apps provide these data to our account holders by means of pie charts and other methods.'

'So, everyone must have a health check-up?' Asks one team member.

Arjun responds saying, 'That a lifestyle assessment is required to determine how much life is there. So, basically, I want to spend money on those who care about their health and family. Are they indulging in habits like smoking, drinking or any other drug intake? Drug intake means regular normal medications also.'

'So, all their health data, doctor visits, prescriptions purchased, junk consumed, and everything else must be kept in their profile and updated using their SSN number. As a result, their health status should also be included in their profile.' 'Can their monthly bank statement be used to track their expenditure on food?'

Only those families who maintain specific levels of good health will be eligible for those special recruitments.

Arjun continues to say 'Why should I care about or spend money on someone who is not concerned about their own health or family?'

The members look shell shocked.

Upon checking the car number, they find out the travels from where it's booked. The travel owner said that one car is booked by an individual and payment was done by him and gave the pickup location. They collected the CC footage of the person, who has done the payment.

The same individual has done the payment at the institution also. Arjun tells him to run a check on his ID. They also find out that she was again dropped at the same place. Arjun tells his officers to try to find out where she might have moved next. If possible, try to gather footage from that location, where she might have left.

About the catering vehicle the officers meet the security guard outside the bank. They come to know that the manager has got promoted and lunch has been arranged for all the staff from the college canteen. The news only came the before day.

Upon asking why he allowed the driver to park the vehicle behind the building. The guard responds by saying that he is a known guy, who has been doing odd jobs here and there with in the campus. So, when he asked to park the vehicle there, he said yes.

Arjun sitting in his car tells them to find out what kind of jobs he has done in the campus and starts to leave from the college.

Arjun checks the collected evidence from the room. He looks at the watch and also one connector device with a different pin which he has never seen before. He tells his team to send the device to the tech team and check what it is used for?

He gets updated that nothing much from the CCTV footages or from the ID checks have come up. Their identities are not matched from any of the sector. Neither any information about the company which sponsored the student. It could be a dummy.

He gets back to the car. Starts to rethink the sequence of events. Trying to understand how are they communicating. None of them is in their database to know their location. How come they have entered or are staying in the city.

Seated in his car Arjun looks clueless. He receives a call from his sister.

'How was your exam?' asks his sister.

'Fine. Not bad,' says Arjun.

'Where are you now?'

'I'm outside.'

'No classes?' She asks.

'During the final semester we have only project work. There are no classes to attend.'

'Ok. Are you eating well?' She continues to ask Arjun.

Hmm.

'Ok then. Take care.'

'You, too. Arjun adds.'

He hangs up the phone.

Starts to drive and leaves from that place.

ONLY ONE MOTTO: EASE OF DOING BUSINESS

Registrations and other processing steps will be taken care by us from now on wards. Make the paperwork as simple as possible. This is the work, this is the capital required, this is the amount of people required to complete the task. Everything has to be decided beforehand.'

'Reduce the number of approvals.'

'How many outside consulting companies are using our own services also? Kindly check it to know their dependency on us. See the old companies are hiring and also paying their employees. Everything appears to be organized but I feel it's still unorganized.'

'Next year most of the tenders are going to come to an end. Let us try to restructure it... Develop a framework for this. I want that to be balanced, so that we don't lose votes from these reputed families or at least the damage from their side won't affect us much.' Arjun elaborated.

The concerned department members in the meeting appear puzzled.

Arjun continues. 'Let us prepare a report stating how much they were earning with the old scenario and now with the present scenario. Calculate the profits they will earn on the margins and different percentages decided by us.'

'All the balance sheets and particularly personal expenditure of these people can be known from their bank accounts. Let us prepare for the argument keeping all these things in view.'

'Let the investments be equal. Specified roles are already identified. Do the recruitment. Let them carry out the work assigned to them. Let the stakeholders get the updates. The numbers are taken care by us. Let us share the profits. Try to make everything organized.'

The team members oblige.

'Concentrate on these three things: Finances, Infrastructure and Technology.'

'Also, keep an eye on the labour laws and make any changes if required for the proposed scenario. Don't forget that everything what we are doing is not only to our people but to other services also- exports and people of other states or someone not registered with us. We want more people to be associated with our company.'

Another question pops up from one of the team members.

In a classroom, Annanya is seated opposite to Arjun, filling out a questionnaire. Arjun keeps staring at her. She looks stunning in blue. He is wearing a sky- blue solid shirt with blue jeans. He instructs her to mark her choices.

The timer has been set for 30 minutes. Midway through, she wonders why these questions are being asked. 'How am I expected to respond?' She asks.

'Simply by reading them'. He chuckles.

Annanya becomes furious.

'I mean just try to read them carefully.' Arjun tries to cover up.

'You might have come across a tricky question. Simply respond to them based on what you have understood. It's a simple activity. Don't be afraid as if your life is dependent on it.'

She continues to answer the questions while Arjun stares in awe at her beauty.

He continues to admire the beauty of the angel in front of him.

Chapter - 6
Still Ringing

The watch is being examined by the technician. The device has four buttons on it. Nothing has been mentioned. One of the buttons is red. One is green, while the other is yellow. The other one being black is unknown. They try to troubleshoot the watch but discover nothing.

He updates the same to Arjun and concludes stating that he'd try to get it back to a basic usage level. Arjun tells him to keep him posted about any new developments.

The tech guy obliges.

'If we acquire all the job descriptions, courses should be tailored based on industry requirements and specializations rather than studying a lot of topics. Create a new curriculum based on these modifications. Frame it based on industry requirements. Experts from industry should also teach. Include that.'

'Based on that information and projected growth, plan for student enrolment in a particular course and the number of jobs that can be created in the future. Calculate that also.'

'Estimate the number of jobs available for each course and create a catalogue for each position. Try to match with the industry requirement. All this data should be known to the student at the beginning of the course, as well as the type of industry in which he or she is interested to work.'

After a few days, the tech guy updates Arjun that the watch is showing just the time and nothing else. Also, if he is pressing that yellow button, numbers are displayed in sequence from ten to one.

The tech guy tried to debug it but couldn't find anything significant. He continues to state that the sequence could be a series of events or a countdown.

Arjun responds saying, "If we assume each team member is holding a watch; how are they all connected?'

'It could be a possibility sir. I have seen these kind of watches sir, they connect only to a predefined network only. They might me using a different network sir. We need to connect to their network or they could be activated by another watch on the network. That could assist us to learn more about its functionality. They can be operated up to a certain radius. All above are possibilities sir, based on our observation.'

'OK!'. Says Arjun.

He ends the call saying, 'Try to look for any other solutions to debug it, if possible'.

The tech guy obliges.

'Institution wise plan for improving the infrastructure. Come from bottom to top. Create a baseline for infrastructure needs in each and every college. I need the current inspection reports of all the institution. Teaching and non-teaching staff requirements also should be covered in our proposal. Start estimating on our budgets now. How much are we going to spend on this?'

'Regarding placements or providing jobs anywhere notification should have a clear job description. Break down their work into smaller tasks to understand how much time is required to complete certain task and how much effort and how much expertise is required to conduct that job?'

'Also, how much pre job industry exposure is required? Do that survey also for a job; develop it before posting the job online. Also pay them accordingly.'

'Physical as well as mental wellbeing is important for the employee. Add in personality testing also to see who fits in along with the existing team. Think about how to inculcate the same into their academics – the same criteria and their learning process. Conduct few psychometric tests before getting into the jobs. Make it compulsory. All these details have to be updated in their profile via their SSN number.'

'After getting the information about future job placements corresponding notification, exam and recruitment schedule should be followed properly and no delays should be there. Look for any particular windows where we can post the jobs suiting the requirement of the industry and the students coming out of the colleges.'

Seated in his college library Arjun examines his bank account balance. 35,000 RC seems to be the current balance amount. He feels the amount to be inadequate.

Closes the laptop and gets back to his house. After the dinner, while seated in his room ideally, thoughts about money, keep running in his mind. He turns off the light and tries to sleep.

At the house inspector Vijay and one of his team members are inside the car watching something in the mobile. The car is parked in front of the house. Other two are inside the house. The normal security guards who always stay at home are at the balcony making rounds. A video plays in the mobile showing some blast.

The officers outside are still moving and they are suddenly shot. Three of them on the floor in a flash. Men in the car try to get down but as they try to open their doors a bullet passes through the door on each side. They again close their doors immediately.

One person starts approaching towards the car; he was earlier positioned as a beggar in front of the temple which is opposite to the girl's hostel. The girls, hostel is situated a few houses away from Meghna's house. From the top floor of the hostel, the lady shoots one cable which anchors to Meghna's house.

The video played in the mobile is that of the blast occurred near the station, which processes the satellite feed of Meghna's house. The equipment established for receiving the feed gets blasted. The operator calls to the CEO to update about the incident. He is furious with them as they should have called the person at the field rather to him. While speaking to the operator, he presses one button beside his bed.

Peacefully sleeping on his bed, Arjun's room starts to light up RED and the sound from his tracker wakes him up. He then calls the CEO but the lines appear to be busy. The satellite operator tries to communicate with Vijay but he couldn't take the call, as he is under control of the guy positioned in front of the car with his gun pointed at him.

The guards inside the house notice what's happening outside through the CCTV monitor. But they are hesitant initially to go outside. They take different positions in the room. One of the guards just then receives a call from the operator explaining the situation. 'Are the mother and the girl aware of the events unfolding outside?'

The lady drifts down through the rope and lands on the corridor and gets ready to enter the house. She ducks down and slowly opens the door and throws in a gas bottle.

CEO calls Arjun to ask him where he is. Arjun replies he has just jumped the wall of his house. 'I tried to reach out to you sir, all lines were busy.' He explains the situation and orders him to reach the location as early as possible.

The guy still aims at the car and the timer in his watch shows 9 minutes remaining. The lady enters the house and the officer who is behind the door punches on her face. They now face each other. They exchange few blows and, in the process, they roll down the steps. While rolling down the sniper lands few more punches on the other lady, breaks the railing of the stairs and falls on the surface in the ground floor.

'Sir, shall we make any curriculum changes in school?' asks one of the spokespersons.

'Not much,' says Arjun.

'If possible, start collecting the information about their interests right from the childhood and they should be aware of these things around them. Also, how technology is shaping in future and all these can be clubbed and integrated to one.'

'Accordingly make those changes in the curriculum. Changes require lot of time. Take one month time. Allot separate team for this job. I want a detailed report after one month. Don't do a lot of changes but try to integrate our plans into the current one.'

'I want the best and brightest students not to leave our company. Start identifying them at early stages and nurture them to take up big responsibilities. If I have to pay more also, I don't mind but maintain a separate record of them.'

Meanwhile another kidnapper who shot the guard stationed at the front side of the house also enters the same way as his partner did. Before entering he places few more sedative bullets into the unconscious guards outside. The timer shows 7 and a half mins.

He enters the house and faces the other officer. In the ground floor, up on their feet again both the women exchange few more blows and the officer is killed by the sniper as a token of revenge.

The sniper lady now takes the steps to go to the bedroom. The other officer is taken down by the second sniper. Now both the snipers approach towards the bedroom. The timer shows 5 mins.

With 5 mins left the person watching the blast starts his car and starts to move from his current location. Meanwhile both of them break the door, to find out that only the mother was there and the girl missing. They start threatening her to tell quickly where her daughter is. They recall that nobody has left the home since dinner. He points his gun towards the mother.

One of the members asks Arjun, 'If everything is done by the company, the processing and registration then where will they get money from other people sir?'

'Let us collect nominal fees for that. If we are collecting all this money and then taxes what is left for them, for themselves, is that money sufficient? That is the reason why these people are getting into illegal methods of earnings.'

'Calculate the expenditure. Estimates the profits as well. Make a good deal with these people. That is what I want. It should look like choice is theirs but their lifestyle should be designed by us from all this data.'

'If those present companies are not willing to come into our new terms, give them a chance to cancel their tenders.

'Sir, we may lose the votes.' He objected.

'How many? Don't simply say we will lose votes. Try to come with an estimated number.' Replied Arjun.

The team members get frustrated with Arjun comments.

'How can he simply tell them to cancel the tender?' Says one team member to another.

'The company will get into a disastrous position if a person like this with no knowledge comes to power. My fate I am sitting here in this group.'

Arjun continues to say, 'If they refuse to support let's bring in more Start-ups – All the financing and investments, I will take care of them.' Most of the spokespersons respond with an unconvincing look on their faces.

Another individual asks, 'Why are we decentralizing sir?

'As I said everything looks organized from outside but for me it looks unorganized. Look into the reason for certain crimes and various illegal things happening. Where there is huge money, crime also follows there. I am trying to keep both those numbers as small as possible.'

'Let me know the percentages of voters, we will lose, if we go this way.'

While Arjun tries to call his boss for the first time he couldn't reach out to him as he is explaining the current situation to the mother. He reminds her of the instructions which were briefed to the girl beforehand in case of occurrence of these kinds of situations.

The mother immediately presses a button on the heart symbol of a doll which is beside the bed lamp. In a pattern of squares on one side of the wall, a hidden door opens behind the bed. She tells Meghna to go past the door. She refuses at first. Very frightened, the mother tries to calm her down. She enters into it and the door closes.

The secretary informs Arjun that other contestants social media account pages are live, but Arjun's team is yet to publish even one post.

Arjun responds that there is time for it. He asks them to concentrate on the work that has been assigned to them.

'Okay Sir.'

'I just wanted to let you know that other teams are starting to establish good relationships with the people. That will help in capturing their attention and developing a relationship with them sir.'

'Follow my instructions.'

'Sure Sir.' She looks disappointed.

Outside near the vehicle, the three men see another car approaching towards them very fast. The driver takes a sharp turn to the left and comes in line with the parked car and stops. Another member from the kidnapper's team gets down from the vehicle and asks his teammate why it was getting late. 4mins were left in his timer.

The girl follows the instructions of the CEO and stops at a point. He tells her to wait at that point until further instructions. The girl says that the place is very shallow and dark. She was very scared right then.

Both of them still threaten the mother to tell the girl's location. She tells her partner to go down and check the entire house. Time is running out. 3 mins left.

Meghna continues to say that she wants to go back to her room. She tells him that she could hear some sounds. She is frightened. CEO tells her to be a bit more patient otherwise she will fall into the hands of the kidnappers. The CEO tells her that they will leave once they will find out that she is not present there. Also, the backup team is on the way. He tells her to be patient and give him a minute.

Her partner gets back to the room and says that he has checked all the rooms also exit points. Nothing suspicious. She observes the entire room and looks at the squares on the wall. 90 seconds left.

Outside the driver says, 'It's getting too late and the back-up team of Vijay could arrive at any time. If my guess is right, by 1 minute they will be here. I will start the vehicle and be ready.' His partner responds with a YES.

Meghna tells the CEO that she can't stay inside for another second. She is completely frightened. The CEO trying to console her, tells her to move forward and open the next door.

'Meanwhile let me think of an alternative.' He says.

Looking at the wall, the sniper doubts that there might be an exit from this pattern. She now places the gun on the mother's forehead and threatens to kill her.

'How much land is available for farming? Ours as well as other people. I want the details- whose ownership- what type of crop- where it is produced, where it has to be transported. How much of the time in a year are we going for farming? Every crop detail I want (all those categories show in that map- along with what type of crops can be irrigated.)

'How much workforce is in agriculture?'

'I need details about production- selling –storage- income. I want all the numbers. How much expenditure has incurred and how much are we earning through agricultural products.'

'Are they maintaining seed quality or not? Don't forget about exports.'

'I want the list of farmers who are registered under our program (land can be theirs or ours). What subsidies are given to the farmers- how much are they earning in real sense. I need analysis of the last 5 years MSP (Minimum Selling Price) from the data. How is our PDS – Public Distribution System currently operated?'

'Also keep an eye on nutritional levels and what people are eating.'

To the staff allotted in this division, Arjun informs the corresponding spokesperson to divide them into two halves. One half to do the earlier mentioned task. Other half to look for solutions or how to prepare better productivity methods.

'I need to know what type of irrigation methods are we using? How much updated are we? List them. Any micro irrigation techniques or crop diversification methods? Any recent technological advancement?'

'Which area is famous for which production and how can we maximize the profits as well as people's satisfaction?'

Next Arjun tells the secretary to arrange meeting with the team dealing with logistics and transportation department. Also asks her to arrange for all the industrial products and other commodities which have to be transported have to be displayed on the big map. He tells her to arrange that graphic also and link them in the map.

She obliges.

The final door opens and CEO tells Meghna to go past through the door. She sees an empty shop with the shutter closed. There is a bag to her right. He tells her to collect it.

He tells her to press the green button near the shutter so that it opens and she can go outside.

She continues to follow his instructions. Opens the shutter. Comes out of the shop. He tells her to get to other side of the road and stop any vehicle coming her way.

The sniper goes out to the corridor to check the situation outside. His other teammates insist him to make it quick. He gets back to the room. In frustration she takes the bed lamp beside the doll and throws it at the wall.

The driver senses few vehicles approaching from the other street.

With great hesitation she comes out of that room and both of them get back to the car. They see another car approaching them. She tries to shot the car tyres but fails.

They leave from their position. The approaching car now takes their place.

Arjun's team members are seen in that car. Inspector Vijay and the other officer gets into this vehicle and goes after the car. They share their current location with Arjun.

'Meghna is on the road waiting for a vehicle.'

'Industry wise – Two wheelers, cars, lorries and other heavy vehicles- Number of green vehicles in each area. List them immediately. Currently most polluted areas in all locations. Also count of vehicles moving in those areas and what could be their future requirement.'

'Coming to logistics- (ROAD, RAIL, AIR, and WATER). How to maximize connectivity from villages to highways and cities? Prepare an action plan for that.'

'Sir for transportation of industrial goods, currently the cost of transportation is less for rail and for road its medium.'

'So, tracks to tyres -how can it be integrated successfully, think of an action plan.'

'How to reduce pollution (what measures) for public use and for company use (services).'

'Logistics division- I want to know how many private parties are involved in the entire process.'

'If we want to reduce pollution we have to concentrate on green power.' Arjun tells the secretary to arrange one meeting with the energy division group. Instructs her to tell them to be prepared with current status of the lightning of all the sectors.

The kidnappers take an immediate right and approaches to a junction and take left. Meghna notices a vehicle approaching her. The CEO is still on the line. She asks him if it is safe to stop the vehicle.

He urges her to stop the vehicle and hand over the phone to the driver but not to speak to him much. She stops the car. The phone's speaker is turned on.

The CEO speaks to the driver "Mister, I want your driving to speak rather than you. Now drive as fast as you can; the location is shared with this number and the girl will guide you. If the vehicle stops or the phone call stops, I will make sure today would be your last day in your life. Don't try to act smart. Just follow the instructions. Drop the girl at the destination. Take your reward and leave.'

'Is that fine for you?'

'Hmm.' The driver responds.

He tells Meghna that one gun is already planted in the bag and that if the driver does anything wrong just shoot him, I will take care of the rest.

The girl obliges.

The chase continues and another car has joined now. Arjun is also seen taking a sharp right and pacing up quickly.

The phone conversation is cut in between. CEO seeks to reconnect. The phone keeps ringing but Meghna isn't taking the call. It's still ringing. He doesn't know what has happened on the other side. He appears tensed.

In a different timeline-

Two unknown individuals conversing over the phone. 'Sir, one of the profiles on your list that you gave me matches with one student named Arjun. Same college and same department.'

'Okay, get him here as quickly as possible.'

Chapter - 7
Money, Gold & Stocks

Arjun is in talks with the power sector people. 'For me the most important thing is the electrification- each and every street should be lightened. Street, city, village – everything should be lightened. Arjun emphasises on this. Estimate for this project and let me know how much it is going to cost.'

'At present how much area is lightened up give me that data also. Project that on the big screen.'

'What are our current investments in green energy?' One of the employee replies with a number.

'Have to be a lot more. Keep it 60-40. 60 renewable and 40 non-renewable Plan and estimate the cost accordingly for that complete electrification project.'

'Coal to renewable and how much GW power is required. Estimate that also. Coal transportation and dependency- imports and exports. I want that data also. Power to most of the infrastructure projects should be from renewable power.'

CEO is yet to connect to Meghna. After a minute it gets connected. The CEO inquires if everything is all right. She says signal issue.

After some time, the car arrives at the CEO's home. He is waiting outside. She exits the vehicle. He greets her and asks her not to worry. 'You're back home my child. Go inside and make a call to your mother. Everything will be fine.' He tells her.

The CEO approaches the car and gets into the car.

Arjun starts looking at the social media profiles of the other contenders. Few points are taken down. After that Arjun has a discussion with all the members related to agricultural department.

'What is the biggest challenge in your study?' He asks.

'Most of them are small land owners,' responds the spokesperson.

'What if we consider them as employees? Let's think in this direction. I think more than 50 percent of the lands are ours right. Make an agreement with other land owners also. Whoever agrees. Consider them also.'

'Prepare a framework for this. Let us take those lands for lease. If they agree to.'

'If our company takes the entire responsibility and takes certain percentage of profits based on each crop. Is that feasible? Prepare a report how can we proceed on this.'

'Besides farming, let's also concentrate on their lives. Now for their basic living and connectivity using technology. How can we connect these villages? Cost of living in those areas and how those areas can be connected to major cities. How their lives can be improved?'

'How to educate farmers; take a look at that also? Plan for connecting those small villages. Also, the existing loans given to the farmers. What's their debt amount?'

Arjun's father instructs him to create a new resume. This sunday, they will meet someone who will be able to refer him for a job. He instructs him to create two resumes. One with gaps and one without any mention of gaps. Arjun complies.

They meet a common friend of his father. Arjun is in his maroon polo tees. He looks at his resume. He asks him about so many gaps. What had he been doing until now. He lectures him about how one should plan their career. His father joins him. He said, 'By this time most of your friends might be settled with a good job. Some of them might be married also. Your father is worried about you.' Arjun quietly listens to him.

'You have studied at prestigious institutions and with your grades you must have qualified for competitive exams also.' He doesn't give Arjun much room to speak. He assures his father not to worry and promises to contact him in a week.

Arjun's father tells him to wait outside the restaurant.

Arjun walks out of the restaurant, disgusted. He is upset because his father has approached someone else for his job. He looks disappointed.

His father comes out after a few minutes. Arjun expresses the same to him that he doesn't like him asking someone else for help. His father asks him to give guarantee that he will get a job in a month, he will stop all this.

'At least you tell me what you want to do with your life.'

Arjun whispers to himself, "Asking me as if you would say a straight yes."

'How many more years will you be like this, jobless and stuck in life? You must move on with your life.' His father adds.

Arjun doesn't speak much. They both depart from the location.

Speaking to the energy division people Arjun tells them to concentrate on these three parameters- RELIABLITY, AFFORDABILTY AND SUSTAINABILTY. 'How many cleaner air days are there in a year, most populated area in the city- How are the pollution levels maintained? Gather that data also.'

'Look for alternatives other than solar, wind like hydrogen, traditional biomass, natural gas. In which areas these alternatives are available so that power can be generated and delivered at that location. Concentrate on this point also.' Instructed Arjun.

'I need an estimation of that power can be generated from each and every resource. What about our transmission and distribution?'

Arjun and the CEO are seated across the table in opposite chairs. Arjun in his very formal attire. The CEO lays three cards on the table. He starts to speak and says since you have accepted my offer; you have the option to choose one of the following as your pay check.

You've got 'MONEY, GOLD and STOCKS'.

Arjun leans forward, pushes all the three cards aside. He takes a piece of paper and places it on the table. The CEO now leans forward to check what Arjun has written on it. The CEO takes the paper and has a look at it.

'This is what you want, Arjun. Really?' He looks surprised.

Arjun responds with a YES.

Surprised by his choice the CEO accepts it.

The CEO approaches the car and gets into the car. The driver turns out to be Arjun and the CEO seems to be relieved now.

Guruji…

CEO compliments him for making it to his house. 'Yes, I did make it.' He inquired if she had any questions. 'Few questions but everything is under control now.'

Arjun continues, 'Its fine that these things happened now. My course will be completed in one and a half months. She might not see me again after that. What if the same thing occurs at the beginning of the course?'

'How could I face her in college?'

He enquires about the other team. Meanwhile he receives a phone call. Inspector Vijay calls to inform him that the kidnapper squad has fled in multiple directions and they are unable to track them down.

The CEO instructs him, 'Make the local police check all the surrounding areas. After that return to the girls' home. Another crew has already been dispatched to the house. Keep me updated.' He ends the call there.

Arjun tells him that he will go to that spot now. The CEO instructs him to first go to his home as there are few hours left for sunrise. Arjun summons his team mates and urges to gather them at 9:30 a.m.

He parks the car in the shed. Closes the shutter and goes back to his home. The time is 5 a.m...

'By road and trucks-what is the average distance covered in a day?'

'300 Km per day sir, which is only 40 percent running sir' responds one of the team members.

'What is the Global Average?'

'500-800 Km per day Sir.'

'So, look for options which would increase our distance also. Once again regulations and certifications in LOGISTICS division- everything taken care by the company itself. I want half of the team to develop IDS-Integrated digital System for logistics services.'

'Also create one platform to integrate all the systems. Trucks must have access to the internet (so whatever areas they are going to move; network has to be covered). Implement 24*7 customer service. Trust can be created with 24*7 emergency services.'

'Sure Sir.'

Arjun and Annanya are in their car. Annanya in her salwar kameez while Arjun is in his green polo T-shirt and jeans. He is in the front seat while she is seated in the rear seat. She is having her lunch. Annanya asks what Arjun is writing. He said that he was working on his last month expenses.

'Let me see them'. She says.

He refuses to show it. 'Say that you will marry me, I will show you.' He adds.

'How much wealth did you add up?' asks Annanya.

'Yours, as well as your family.' She adds.

'Leave my father's wealth. Whatever I acquired, I will put it all in your name. Will you marry me?' says Arjun.

'Not like that, I don't want your money. You don't seem to be working anywhere, so how do you make money and sustain? I was just curious about it.'

Arjun tells her to first respond with a yes, and then he will answer all her questions.

'Don't we have something else to talk?' She smiles and tosses the spoon at him.

At noon the entire crew attends to the rituals of the deceased officer. A few officers have minor injuries. Arjun goes to college and signs across his name in the register. Later he drives his car to the ceremony place. He remains in the car and witnesses the rituals being performed. He does the same at the cemetery.

He recalls how she was assigned to his team in the early days. Good memories resurface. He misses her badly. Arjun gets a call from his boss; he asks if he wants to add anyone to the team. Arjun answers with a NO.

Meghna gets back to her house. Vijay's and Arjun's team members gather at the residence. While Arjun is outside the college library, the CEO pays a visit to the residence to consoles both the mother and the daughter. The time is now 7 p.m.

Following the visit, the CEO begins the meeting by asking if there are any leads. Vijay responds by explaining that, 'The sniper 1 who was a female had stationed inside the room of the girl's hostel. She joined the girl's hostel 10 days back. She went back to her hometown after completing the formalities and only returned yesterday. This is as per the statement of the hostel warden.'

Vijay continues to say that even the homeless person who was stationed at the temple in the evening wasn't the regular one.

'Didn't the satellite operator notice?'

'No, Sir, the family went for a movie yesterday, therefore the satellite guy was stationed at the mall.'

'What about the second sniper?'

'He was outside our view. The distance is significantly long sir.'

'Any footage from hostel?'

'Yes Sir, images are already sent to office sir.'

'Did you run a background check on her?'

'Yes Sir.'

'No leads Sir. Nothing from our database.'

'His response would be always NO.' Arjun steps in. 'Why to ask him all these questions?'

Vijay stumbles and responds with NOT LIKE THAT Sir.

'What about their exit?' CEO continues to ask.

Arjun interrupts once more, asking, "What's the point, sir?"

'What would his response be?'

Arjun is ordered by the CEO to keep quiet for a while.

'What about the explosion at the satellite receiver's office?'

'We are trying to find it out sir.'

The CEO adds, because the equipment is not readily available, it will take months to reestablish.

Arjun inquires with the CEO about possible replacements.

All other similar modules are now engaged in other high-security assignments. So..

'Understood Sir!' Says Arjun very frustratingly.

'It's all right, Sir. Can we call off the meeting? It's pointless to sit here and keep discussing. I want all of the officers to safeguard the girl from now onwards. I'll handle the investigation part.'

'We have no idea who they are. How do they communicate? Where are they staying? What are their plans? If you are able to find the answers to these questions. Let me know.'

'I don't want any more attacks. Neither do I want to lose you guys.'

'Sitting here and having discussions is a waste of time.'

All the members are shell shocked by Arjun's words. Few frightened.

'Take Care. Everyone.'

'Bye, Sir.'

CEO tells them not to be concerned about Arjun and to focus on their work. He also departs from that place.

Arjun instructs his secretary to schedule a meeting with the PR team and the members of the social media team.

'Depending on other teams' posts. Choose a window which has the potential to develop more viewership and engagement with the public. Our posting frequency would be twice a week. So let me know which slots are available.' He orders the team members.

Chapter - 8
Got Caught!

Arjun restarts the investigation from his perspective, attempting to connect the dots.

He talks to the student about that project over the phone. The two officers make him feel comfortable. Arjun wants him to explain everything about his idea and how it came to be financed. The student typically repeats himself like previously.

Meanwhile, one of the officers continues to examine the investigation file, and the student identifies the deceased individual and informs him that he saw him at the institute. He was also there in the manager's room when he inquired about the sponsorship.

Arjun becomes excited and instructs his two officers to go to the institute and speak to the manager.

Arjun along with his friend goes to the substation and request to load data for their project. His friend approaches them for information, while Arjun looks around for any clues. He returns after failing to get any clues.

From there, he proceeds to see Vikram who is at the office of his student's club. The same place where the exhibition is conducted. Vikram is completing some paperwork to close the scholarship account as they will be leaving next month. Arjun looks for clues but finds nothing unusual.

The officers paid a visit to the institute and showed the photograph to the manager. The manager responded by saying that the guy approached him about making a connector pin. He said, 'The pin and shape must be distinct from those currently in the market. He handed me the design and instructed me to manufacture ten of those. He would take care of the remaining components.'

They inquired as to when he first approached him. It was possibly during the second week of the December.

'How was the payment done?'

'He paid in cash, sir.'

The same message is delivered to Arjun. Arjun instructs them to collect any material related to that device.

Arjun visits each location and ensures that all CCTV footage has been obtained so that no information has been overlooked. He is still in his car, with a dejected look on his face.

He keeps thinking on how they are executing their plans. He believes that if he can crack it, he will immediately know how they are communicating and where they are staying. He has a feeling that he is missing something. He visits the secret office to retrieve the communication device. He has a look at it and sends the same to the tech team.

'During another meeting, if we take the whole responsibility providing all the requirements and still incur losses, can we survive?' Arjun asks the opinion of the remaining team members what they feel about the situation whether they support his idea or not.

'If we still do all this and suffer losses, how can we deal with it? What are the best chances to suffer losses? I want the information on how we can lose the profits.'

'Sir mostly it depends on climatic conditions such as rainfall and the seed quality.' Arjun replies back by saying, 'Do you want me tell how much produce we lost due to insufficient storage facilities.'

'Which crop is placed, where and how much water is required. Whether water is available or not? Depending on monsoon how can we control rain? Monsoon at those places- How are they for the past 3 years. How to get correct percentage of rainfall and avoid floods?'

'What should be done to maintain the rainfall within limits? Prepare a report. In case of floods, are there proper drainage systems? When are you going to submit all the reports?'

'Speed up guys.'

Arjun's father arranges an interview. His father instructs him to respond carefully and not to speak too much.

Arjun shows up for the interview. He is dressed up in a white formal shirt and black trousers. After a few questions about his engineering field, he is asked the same question again.

'Why are there so many gaps? Why has he taken so many breaks?'

Arjun responds by saying, 'I believe that in addition to our career, we needed to explore life also sir.'

'Yes, I agree. However, at your age, your peers are succeeding in life, here you are still looking for a decent job.'

'Sir, we have been onto something or the other since we were little. I've never taken a break. I felt as if I needed one. That's all, sir. I just wanted to experience life in many other ways.'

The interviewer appears unimpressed.

'How do you envision yourself in this organization after 5 years?'

'At this point, sir, I haven't given much of a thought about it. I'm trying to stay in the present moment.'

The interviewer becomes enraged. He asks, 'When do you think then?'

'It's not only about the job description, sir. I'm not familiar with the culture or the work environment here. There are already people working here. We always talk about work but there are many other things that are important in a work place.'

'Work wise I will not compromise sir. I will give my 100 percent sir. At this point of time, I am not thinking much sir. Kindly ask the same question after 2-3 months. I will definitely let you know sir.'

'Nobody will stay here forever sir. I'm sure you're aware of this, sir.'

The interviewer locks his gaze on Arjun for 5 seconds.

'We'll let you know about our choice in a week, Arjun. You may now leave the room.'

'Thank you very much, Sir.'

Arjun comes out of the building. He immediately calls his father, informs him that the interview is done. He departs from that location.

The tech guy updates that it could be a 3- part device- They got part one of the device from the dead guy. That is a communication device. Information about part two which is the pin connection, we got it from the institute. We should know where the third one is placed. Power source is additional.'

'We don't know where they are using the whole combination. It's a kind of communication device. The pin connector isn't the regular one.'

Arjun keeps thinking, from where he can get his next clue.

'Let us now turn our attention to the industries? How many new plants should we establish based on our estimates? I'd like to see a list of all OEMs (ORIGINAL EQUIPMENT MANUFACTURERS).'

'Where do we acquire the equipment to make each part or do we make it by ourselves? How much does it cost? I'd like to know everything about the new plants that we are planning and how long it will take to set them up?'

'How are payments made to the third parties? What are the gaps?'

'One thing, why we are doing all this?'

'It is to provide facilities for our people and on the other hand based on the market scenario which gap can be filled so that it is profitable for the company.'

Arjun receives a call from a friend informing him that all his classmates are going to the showroom of the car that was advertised a few months ago.

Arjun isn't very eager to meet them but for a change he considers going out. He leaves for the showroom with his friends, keeping his stuff in the library locker.

They arrive at the location. His friends are all excited to see the many models on show.

Arjun cautiously walks around and enters the assembly plant. He meets a mechanic there. They had a brief talk and are now underneath a car. He is modifying the same car according to the buyer's desire.

Arjun examines the inside layout. His friends eventually call him as they are leaving. They leave from that place.

He goes back to college. Picks up the bag from the locker. Something hits him. Packs his bag and leaves the library immediately.

He visits the secret office and collects the pin and the connector from there. Connects them together. Examines the pin.

He makes a call to someone and asks, "Bro, are you still there?"

'Yes,' says the person on the other end.

'I am coming there. Wait for me.'

He runs to the mechanic in the showroom. He's still underneath the car. Arjun gets down and examines the slot beneath the steering wheel, where the same pin has already been kept.

He enquires about a pin connection and its purpose. The mechanic stated that the device was included with the vehicle. He hasn't made any changes to it. He is completely unaware of it.

He requests for a ride from the mechanic.

The mechanic hesitates at first, but eventually gets one key and hands it over to Arjun. He goes for a ride outside the shed. Stops the vehicle a bit far from the shed. Inserts the connecting device to that pin and the device gets powered.

Some of the device's indicators begin to blink. Arjun gets excited. He parks the car back in the garage.

'We all knew that there are stages GENERATION – TRANSMISSION – DISTRIBUTION. On the consumer side do we need any updates on smart metering? I need the details of the subsidies given to costumers for encouraging renewable power.'

'Are we considering any fines to boards for not meeting objective in renewable energy implementation?' 'Plan that also.'

'From a business standpoint, I'd like to know the average cost of supplies and the average revenue generated. Create framework for long-term partnerships with individuals as well as businesses.'

Arjun tells the spokesperson, 'Something keeps running in the back of his mind; with the new changes in policies, can we acquire votes from these people? Think about it.'

'Like mobile sim, can we change the power flow from one power producer to another by placing a switch so that if regulations are not met we can disconnect their line. Think along those lines.'

'Sure Sir.'

'Forgot to say, particularly in villages concentrate mostly on renewable power. Make sure that rainfall is maintained at good levels for coming years. Did any team posted about the power issues?'

'No Sir.'

Arjun is sleeping on the terrace. In the dark with his black polo T-shirt on. He suddenly wakes up as Annanya continues to tickle his feet. She gives a cute smile. Arjun asks her what happened. She asks him, 'What is love?'

'For this you woke me up ah?'

'Tell me Arjun what does love actually means to you?' She asks him once again.

'Not right now. I'll let you know at the right moment.' He closes his eyes once again.

Annanya looks disappointed.

He shuts his eyes and falls asleep but he wakes again. This time at his office. He gets up from the couch. He heads towards the refrigerator. He opens it and takes out the bottle. Takes a glass and places it along the bottle. He looks at the bottle once again.

A notification sound from the desktop prompts him to return to the table.

The key is returned to the mechanic. He hugs him in joy and leaves from the place. He contacts his boss as he gets back into his car. Tells him to meet him at their usual location in half an hour.

When they meet, he tells him that he needs one of those car models.

The boss inquires as to what happened to the existing one, which has been fully upgraded recently. Also, this one is a luxury model. 'What will you do with a luxury model?' Asked the boss.

Arjun explains the situation.

He shows the device and asserts, 'The tech person must crack the full code in order to understand exactly what this equipment is capable of, for which he requires one car to collect the entire unit.'

The boss agrees. He is overjoyed with Arjun's progress. He says that this is why he hired him. He has complete faith in him that he will find a solution one way or the other.

I'm running out of time. Need to get back home immediately. I'll contact you later. They both depart from their location.

'Are you adding the machinery available at those places? How much investment is required in coming years for a new machine at each of the locations. So, crosscheck the present use of machines and based on that data, let's decide how much we can spend on this.'

R&D units in Farming and Agriculture. Where are they located?

'What types of jobs can we create in agriculture?' Arjun tells the spokesperson to give another team this task.

'Like a simple corporate job is done- travel for the farmers to their lands - sheds during summer- water availability for crops as well as for people. What all facilities can be provided if they under our branch? List them.'

'If we provide everything and if the yield is good how can we share the profits? If there is a loss how much money should we spend or give them so that their livelihood should not be affected. I need an estimation of all these. Take data related to amount lost in agriculture sector in the past 4-5 years and analyse the amount in case of a catastrophe.

After reaching his home he calls his team members and orders them to get the list of people who had purchased the car. Their location as well as the buyers who availed that movie offer.

'Which films did they see after purchasing the car?' 'Which places did they visit? I need all of the information ASAP. Run a background check on all the buyers. Let me know if you come across anything suspicious.'

'By tomorrow morning at 10 a.m. all that information should be in the mail.'

'What about Income from Non-Farm Sector- DIARY, CATTLE, REARING AND FISHERIES.'

'Arrange a meeting with the staff who are expertise in these areas.'

'How can we integrate solar and other resources for production? Ethanol, biodiesel and other local fuels so that electricity can be produced at the local areas only.'

Once again, a few employees discussed that he always tells us to do the work. Is he really thinking about the funds? Whether the funds allotted to them will be sufficient or not?

The following day Arjun gets the car he wanted. He sends the device and the car to the tech guy. By noon Arjun receives the information he wanted from his team. After reviewing the data, he instructs them to keep an eye on all the owners and also on ticket bookings this week.

'Keep me posted' says Arjun.

After having his dinner, Arjun receives a call from the tech person who informs him that the device contains a code than can automatically hack into few networks with particular encryption systems.

Fantastic guys. Arjun gets excited.

'If possible, get the names of the service providers names they are using.'

The tech guy further explains that after getting into private network it can create a meeting room where people from different locations can enter the meeting online.

Arjun appreciates their efforts and end up by saying to look for more information.

He makes a conference call to his team members and instructs them to visit all the malls and theatres immediately where tickets were booked earlier.

'I'd like to see the blueprints for all of the malls. Particularly the parking lots and exit points. What are the safest places for them to flee if they know they are being watched?'

'Come on boys, we have a big job ahead of us. I want everyone to buckle up. There will be no breaks or shifts. We should catch those guys this Friday.'

'Keep me posted.'

The next day Arjun visits all the malls by himself.

His boss calls him, 'Are you resting?'

'Yes Sir.'

'Your log data isn't suggesting the same.'

'Nothing like that Sir.'

'Other contestants are taking breaks except you.'

'You've been inside, for longer than I anticipated.'

'Yes Sir. Feel like going for a run.'

'Then go now.'

'Not now Sir.'

'My job ain't finished.'

'I'll be monitoring your vitals as well.'

'Take care of yourself son.'

'Sure Sir.'

A group of people bring in an individual into a secret room with the face covered. He is forced to sit in the chair and is cuffed now. The men leave the room leaving the abducted man alone with their boss. He is revealed and the individual appears to be Arjun. He is dressed in white and black.

Chapter - 9
Kill For Kill

'ROADWAYS- (National Highways, State Highways, Division Highways, Village Roads)-What are our current projects and future plans. All the terms and conditions of the projects allotted to contractors will be same as discussed earlier.'

'Another section should concentrate on-border roads, International highways, express ways.'

'Prepare a framework concentrating on future of logistics. Consider traffic management, fuel expenses, profit margins, customer service, driver rotation, use of technology and transportation costs.'

'Look for supply chain management, inventory management, expansion, and vendor management on the distribution side. Also, truck drivers should be paid on time.'

'How many jobs can we create in this division? Discuss with your team members. Make a presentation and let's discuss in the next meeting.'

Annanya and Arjun are seated in their car. She asks whether he smokes or drinks alcoholic beverages.

Arjun responds with a no.

She asks him why doesn't he.

'Over the last few years, I've realized that my lifestyle and ideology or belief systems started to drift from my parents' belief systems or the family as a whole.'

'So'

'As a result, my happiness cannot be their happiness and their grief cannot be entirely mine. Our approach to things as a family has become diverse.'

'So'

'I'll never be able to make them happy with what I do, nor will they be entirely satisfied with my life. I can't give back anything to my family.'

'But there is something else I could.'

'What is it?' She asks him.

'It has the potential to impact everyone in equal measure.'

'ILLNESS. Bad Health!'

'After all that they have done to me over the years, the only thing I can give back to my family is my health. Both my physical and mental wellbeing.'

'That's the only thing I can give back to my family.'

'Good Mind. Good Sleep. Good Health.'

'Acha!' She says and continues to have her lunch with a smile on her face.

Until now in 15 malls cum theatres tickets were booked. Arjun tells them to remove 2 theatres as the exit points and basements are not feasible to plan such activities.

There are only 13 malls left. Arjun advises them to research the ISP's that these malls use. This number must be reduced. Got to shortlist them quickly.

By Wednesday, all ten car owner's tickets had been purchased. Arjun receives the information.

Arjun looks into the list again. Considers which location would be more suitable for the guys to meet. He has no idea how many men are planning to attend.

He then has a second thought. What about the water servicing? He instructs his employees to review all previous bookings to determine how many times each car was water serviced. Is there a pattern in the allocation of this service?

'Make an effort to obtain that information. Guys, be cautious with your approach.'

'Look into AQUAPONICS- combination of AQUACULTURE AND AGRICULTURE FORESTS and other area coverage and value- added products are also important- Tribes and sentiments of that culture. Don't forget about them.'

Arjun arranges one meeting with all the spokespersons.

'How much of implementation is possible with the budget allotted to us. How many targets can be met? Approach it realistically once the entire survey is done. Then based on priority as well a as considering votes allot the budgets. Try to maintain balance. Discuss with the team and present your considerations to me. Then we will take the final call.' He elaborated.

'Not every time water servicing is done sir. The company agreed to provide the service once a month, which implies that if the automobile visits the mall four times a month, it will be washed once.' Replied the officer.

'Sir we noticed one pattern,' says another officer.

'What is it?'

'Only during six instances, it happened.'

'Go ahead.'

'This is the 11th week sir. So, since 10 weeks until this point of time, only six times, owners of the same 6 cars were booked to the shows at the same location and also the show timings were pretty much similar.'

'So, there is a possibility for them to meet on those instances. Also, their team strength could be 6.' Arjun adds up.

'Check those dates with the dates when we were attacked. Those dates might be near to the attack dates.'

The officer checks it and gets back. 'You are right sir. Few times sir.'

Arjun is ecstatic by the accomplishments of his team members.

'Fantastic guys.'

'So, how about this week? Let's finally narrow down the options and figure out if they'll meet this week or not.'

They respond that tickets have been reserved for this week as well.

Similar pattern is followed this week also. Timings are also very close in-fact.

'Good job guys. Give me details of those locations and the car owners. To be on the safer side keep an eye on the other cars too. Also, the multiplexes they are heading to.'

Arjun himself inspects every location once again.

Each team is assigned to a mall. They are aware of the show's schedule.

Meanwhile the kidnappers are stationed at their hiding place and are all set to make their way to the malls.

'Who are our partners? Technical partner, Operation and maintenance partner and financial partners? How do you attract investors? Have you explored that?'

'Any alternative fuel for cars. Did you consider Methanol? Big Industries how much power must be generated so that they can expand? What are their future needs?'

'What are the plans for the four mega factories? Locate places that are environmentally friendly.

1. Solar PV module manufacturing facility

2. Energy storage factories

3. Production of green hydrogen

4. Fuel Cell Manufacturing Facility'

'Problems with renewables is that we need rare earth metals Lithium, cobalt and copper. There are also mining and environmental risks. If possible, look for alternatives. If there are any alternatives that can be implemented right away consider them; otherwise push it to the future.'

'Until now electricity requirements have been calculated for domestics, industries and agriculture. What about other fields such as communication or information technology?'

Arjun's father asks him whether he has given the salary to his mother.

'I'll give. I will.' Arjun responds.

His father is reading the newspaper while Arjun is having breakfast. Chutney falls on his blue polo tees leaving a mark. Hearing their conversation, his mother comes from the kitchen.

His mother asks him whether he wants to give it or not.

'Not like that maa.'

'For example, if I give an 'X' amount for the next three months and then come back one day and ask for a certain amount that could be more or less than what I gave, will you give me the amount without asking questions?'

'What are you talking Arjun?'

His father is furious with him.

'It is preferable to discuss about overall income. How much we are getting? Current expenditure and expenditure later on, how much is expected. How much should I contribute monthly? Don't you think that I should have an idea about all this?'

Both his parents are listening patiently.

Arjun's father interrupts, saying, "All these years, I've never questioned her on how she handles everything at home; just a month into the job, you're asking these many questions."

Nobody here is dependent on your salary. If you want to give the money to your mother, do so; otherwise leave it. Don't ask stupid questions.

He throws the newspaper onto the sofa and walks towards the bedroom.

Arjun's mother questions why he is saying all this.

'Maa, your record-keeping procedure differs from mine. I'm not implying that your methodology is incorrect; rather I'm trying to convey that our processes are different.'

'I am not an ATM machine maa to give a certain amount every month. If I get an overall picture, then only I can plan accordingly. How much to earn, how much to save and think about other economics.'

'As a son, do you want me to think that my responsibility is only to give my salary and not ask any further questions? Can't we sit and discuss about the things I mentioned above.'

'So, you don't want to give your salary?' She asks him once again.

'Not like that maa. That is not my intention.'

'You are not able to understand what I want to tell.'

'One thing I can say, you already have my cheques signed with you. You can withdraw any amount you want, no need to tell me as well.'

Her mother still has a puzzled look on her face.

He leaves from that place.

'End-to-end encryption is available and will remain so in the future. Set a limit on the number of SIM cards that an individual can register. Make it three. It is mandatory to link all these details to their SSN. The same applies to email addresses also.'

'Login for all social media handles should be linked with these phone numbers only. Make sure that the name of the account is automatically set up to be the same as the one linked with their SSN.'

'Try to develop a digital family tree in the background based on their activity and connectivity using our AI tools. Just try to keep an eye on activities of various groups created on our social media handles.'

Before going to bed, Arjun's mother to her husband, 'You should not have reprimanded him. Is that really necessary?'

Father replies, 'First let him settle down. Then he will be able to take the responsibility.'

'Why all this ?' There is still time for it.' He adds. However, the mother continues to speak.

Arjun's father interrupts, stating that he knows the mother and son are always on the same page.

Now she adds up saying, "That is why I refuse to intervene between father and son. Only to end up listening all this."

'It's enough.'

'I have lot of work in the morning. Let me sleep. Please switch off the lights.'

The lights are turned off.

They are aware of the show's schedule. All the teams are placed at their respective locations. At Arjun's location, they notice one lady getting into the car. Everything is progressing as planned at the other locations as well. They have located the members also.

Now all the members are in the meeting.

The CEO orders that at any cost he wants all leads to be captured tonight.

The meeting has concluded. The lady begins to exit the parking lot. They gradually begin to follow her. She senses she is being followed and alters her course. Arjun and his men force her way to an abandoned retail mart.

The supermarket has two entrances, one in front and one at the back.

His teammates are stationed at the door. They closed the front doors. Arjun enters the mart through the rear door while the lady is trapped inside.

They get into a fight. After a while, Arjun exits the supermarket from behind telling his boys that they may now speak to her and that he is departing from there.

They go inside. His teammates are taken aback to see that lady dead with plenty of blood on the floor. With that state, they couldn't see the body. They summon the medical staff.

Arjun limps slowly and makes a phone call to one person. He informs that he will meet him in 15 minutes.

Arjun urges everyone to stop working since one of their employees had questioned him.

'One of your coworkers has posed a query about me. Why should everyone accept his proposals? What if the majority of people disagree with us? How are we going to get people to vote for us?'

Arjun responds by saying, 'With the kind of regulations in our states and the majority of our resources and money being controlled by one organization, do we have any other choice but to follow these regulations?'

Manager. Logistics Department.39 years old. Married. Two children. 13years of Service. Arjun checks the bio data of the individual.

'Ask your parents or grandparents, what the people who founded this company accomplished for the states and what challenges they encountered. Then ask yourself- Where are we now?'

'I'm not claiming that everything is perfect here.'

'Let me revisit your profile. Good investments. Good savings. What do you want out of life, sir? Do you feel content with your life? Do you have a sense of accomplishment? Are you fully content with your life and experience joy in what you do?'

'Are you able to sleep peacefully?'

'I'm not looking for an answer from you, sir. But do you have an honest answer for yourself? I can provide you few links and statistics about how people live in our neighbouring states.'

'With such big capital and investments just imagine how your future will be. Above everything, our children's future. It's for our future generations.'

'I know that coming big day all my team members will also vote. Your choice doesn't change my perception towards all of you. It is entirely up to you whether you believe or not. But one thing is certain: whether I win or lose, I won't bow down that easily.'

'All my decisions are taken with integrity and honesty and are in the best interests of all the members of the organization and the people of this state. Don't worry about the votes. There is still time to think about the votes. Just finish your present work.'

Signing off.

Everybody gets back to work.

Arjun gets frustrated and approaches for the bottle again. He struggles to resist the impulse to open it. Tries to control himself. He places the bottle back in the fridge. Returns to the desk.

Arjun meets his doctor. Arjun is bleeding from a few cuts on his body. He is drugged and the doctor begins stitching the cuts. He asks the doctor how long he needs to rest. The doctor says he'll give him an injection and that he'll need to sleep for 12 hours.

He calls his mother and informs her that he will not be returning home tonight due to his project work and that he will return in the morning.

The doctor continues to perform his duties. He gives the injection and instructs Arjun to rest.

Arjun receives calls from the CEO.

He is upset and outraged at Arjun once more. He inquires as to what he has done. 'Do you know that we missed on other leads at the malls? And what happened to the lady?'

'I got the photographs.'

'32 cuts.' The speaker is turned on. The doctor has a puzzled expression on his face.

'32 cuts, how could you possibly do this? You're gradually turning into a monster.'

'Who made me like this Sir?' Arjun replies.

Arjun continues stating that he desired vengeance for the killing of his fellow officer.

'So that's why you diverted her to that location rather than following her all the way to her house.'

Arjun gradually becomes unconscious.

Chapter - 10
The Countdown

The boss gets frustrated as once again they have their backs against the wall. There are no clues, but there is a lot of damage and violation of rules.

'What will happen if the high command finds out about this? Are you there Arjun?'

The doctor takes the phone and explains the situation.

The CEO instructs the doctor to notify Arjun to reach out to him, once he is up and going.

'Is there a place where people can file a complaint related to the digital world?'

'Yes Sir.'

'I require all the specifics of such cells. How many complaints are being filed? How long does it take to solve them? What kinds of problems are emerging? How many are monetary in nature?'

'I need those specifics right away.'

'Which areas have higher crime rates, and what is the likely cause?'

'How many police stations are there? What is the current public police ratio? I'd like to know the locations of all the police stations. Post them on the big screen. Also, all personnel data.'

ZONES, RANGES, DIVISIONS, SUBDIVISIONS/CIRCLES, POLICE STATIONS, AND OUTPOSTS. All of this should be highlighted on the big screen.

In the morning Arjun makes his way slowly to his home. He informs his mother that he intends to sleep for a while and then go to college in the afternoon.

He is able to conceal his scars and pain. He goes upstairs to his room and falls asleep once more.

He returns to the medical facility in the afternoon to have his vitals checked.

He takes a few more medications and decides to sleep for a while. He instructs the doctor to notify the CEO that he has arrived at the location.

In the evening, the CEO arrives. He informs Arjun that they discovered 32 incisions on her body. 'Are you insane?'

'Let's keep that discussion for another day sir.'

Arjun feels that it's time for him to get head- to- head with those guys.

'Make your moves slowly Arjun.' CEO tries to cool him down.

Arjun doesn't listen to that.

'Sir, at the end of the day you need clues.'

'Take this watch and send it to the tech guy. Your team has failed on numerous occasions until now. Concentrate on that issue, rather on me. Instruct them to search for any clues at those sites and their final exit point.'

'Let me sleep for a while. I shall return in two days.'

'I need to be back home by 9 PM. Project work is also unfinished.'

He closes his eyes.

CEO looks at Arjun and feels helpless. He tells the doctor to keep him updated on his condition and departs.

'What about phone manufacturing and cellular technology which are two critical components. Apply the same rules that we covered earlier. Our current production and future targets. Is it possible to get our competitors numbers as well?'

'I want to see the technology footprint in all our sectors, particularly rural places.'

Arjun and Annanya are seated in the car. She opens one small cabinet inside the car and find out Arjun's family photos.

She looks at them. Arjun advices her to keep it inside but she doesn't.

'You never tell me about your family. How is your equation with your mother and father?'

'These are your childhood family photos. Aren't there any recent ones?'

He looks at her with a pause. She saw tears welling up in his eyes. He gets down the car.

She also gets down and goes to the other side.

'Arjun what happened?'

'With lot of hopes our parents raise us expecting that we would accomplish something in life and succeed in life. The happiness which they had while raising me for past 28 years, I returned it only with double the years of pain and despair.'

She tries to console him. But he continues to weep.

'Seeing them now always reminds me of the pain I caused them all these years. I'm not sure if I'm a good human being or not, but I'm definitely not a good son.'

'No parent should have a son like me.'

Looking at those photos he says that his parent's happiness ended with these memories.

Annanya attempts to comfort him. He wipes his eyes. He usually doesn't like to be consoled. She opens the car door and tells him to get inside.

He gets into the car as does she.

'I think you're running late. Have your lunch.'

'I am sorry, Arjun.'

'It's ok.'

'Leave it.'

'What are your plans this evening? She tries to cheer him up.'

'Guys I need your response right away for the next thing I'm about to say.'

'How many news stations are there?'

'Three Sir.'

'Who is in charge of them?'

'Directly or indirectly things are managed by our CEO's family members Sir.'

'Right. I want to simplify everything and make it only one channel.'

'What do you think?'

'Sir, it has the potential to cause a major rift within the family as well as among the stakeholders?'

'Yes. Do you have a backup plan in place for such a disaster? Damage control.'

'Think. Think.'

'Make it one channel from our side. if they want, let them team up with others private parties outside our organization to have multiple ones.'

When two watches are placed near each other, they become powered up. The tech guy updates the same to Arjun. They try to debug the new watch.

The tech guy adds up saying that like malls they are communicating via a distinct network. They realized they were communicating by pressing the yellow button.

When a user pushes the yellow button, a number appears which may serve as a countdown for a series of events.

'Can we find out who is linked in this network?'

'No, Sir.'

'But Sir, going by the history, numbers from 10 to 2 are displayed on the screen. The numbers 10 and 8 came from the deceased person's watch while this device produced nine, seven, and three.'

'How about the remaining numbers?'

'6,5,4,2 Sir.'

'Each number originated from a different device.'

'Four more devices?'

'Yes, sir.'

'Then their team may consist of six members. Am I right?'

'Yes, sir.'

Arjun seems surprised.

'How many people were on their team during the second attack?'

'4 Sir.'

'Four persons, one of them has already died. Still, the count is five.'

'So, someone else has been running the network for them all along. Perhaps not in this field. From the outside, he or she may be their leader as well or could be at the location itself.'

'Another login reveals that a ten-minute timer was enabled on the day of the second attack. Just a timer nothing like a countdown for a series of events.'

Arjun asks the tech guy if they can use these watches to track their location.

'No, Sir.'

'How many people visited the malls?'

'4 Sir.'

'How come it's 4. It should be five, right?'

'That suggests he didn't visit that location. If he hasn't visited the malls. How did he communicate with the other members?'

Even after gathering all of this information, Arjun still has a puzzled look on his face.

ZONES, RANGES, DIVISIONS, SUBDIVISIONS/CIRCLES, POLICE STATIONS, AND OUTPOSTS. All of this should be highlighted on the big screen.

'I'd want to see a list of the different wings of these services. All of the services available to an individual should be listed on their SSN login. They should be aware of the contact information for the police officer in charge and the lawyer to approach in any situation.'

'Consider categories like criminal investigation, traffic police, outside patrolling, human rights, reserved forces, fire, military, railway, bodyguard and security, Traffic, law and order. Weaponry, forensic.'

'I want a presentation explaining how all these departments work? Keep me posted if I missed anything.'

Arjun interacts with farmers and heads of the villages regarding rural electrification, which is part of his post-graduate thesis. He also pays a visit to the fields.

He gets a call from the CEO.

'Arjun what happened to that device? Is there any update?'

'No, Sir, I am in a village. I came here to work on my project.'

'How are you funding your project?'

'You seem to be traveling more these days. How much money do you still have in your account? Is that sufficient? Do you need any?'

'It's sufficient, Sir. I'll call you later.'

Arjun starts to imagine the sequence of events. With the help of the CCTV footage, he tries to visualize the sequence of events.

He receives a copy from the tech person that includes the history of the buttons pressed and the time interval between each one.

Number ten is before the deceased person exits the stalls.

'I'm not sure about number 9, but it's pressed by the lady. Think about it later.'

When he opens the back gate lock, he presses number eight.

'Number 7 was again by the lady. No idea. The time was noted down.'

According to the activities and time schedule, number 6 might represent the girls arriving at the exhibition. A new person provided an update because the dead guy is no longer following them.

Now the girls are inside. Number 5 could represent the device that injects.

Number 4 comes from a new person. No idea.

Number three, she removes the breaker. The power is gone.

Arjun notices something in one of the footages. As soon as the power goes out, the exhibition halls go dark, but one lighting board with the event name remains on. How come?

He views the clip again. When the number 4 is pressed he attempts to synchronize the time. Three different colors of tiny LEDs are placed around the board. When you press the number 4, the green color is highlighted.

He calls one of his associates and instructs him to check if the board is still present in the exhibition hall.

He tells the other officer to go to the substation and ask what the lady did during her visit. Very detailed. Every movement of hers.

Meanwhile, he examines video footage of the board attempting to sync with other numbers to look for additional possibilities.

He receives a call from an officer at the substation informing him that she has handed them a wall clock as a present from the firm. Arjun tells him to deliver it to their location.

From the exhibition hall, the officer calls Arjun and informs him that the board is still present.

The wall clock and the board are bought to one location. Both the things have similar pattern or arrangements of lights inside. The officers are in their usual location in the parking lot besides Meghna's building.

Arjun instructs them to share a photo of the same.

He orders them to dismantle them. He suggests that there could be a timer or device attached to them. Check them out once.

The officers respond by noting that there is a similar device attached to both the things. Arjun instructs them to submit it to the tech guy.

He informs the IT person of the situation and instructs him to stay updated.

The officer provides a full explanation to Arjun about the lady's activities at the substation.

'Only one channel how would you like to proceed, sir?'

Everything will be referred by a single name.

'News is divided into several categories: journalism, investigations, crime, politics, business, arts, fashion, education, sports, science, health, and entertainment.'

'Each branch will function as a news channel but under the same parent's name. Plan accordingly and let me know about any change to be done. Nobody will lose their present job but a shift in how things are managed.'

'Even though VPN access is available, ensure that all IP addresses for each and every login are recorded, as well as the location of that IP address.'

'Whether the location is showing within our sectors or not? Keep an eye on it.'

'Sir, many regulations have been implemented in recent years but we are yet to get a complete hold of this.'

'Achaa' 'Details about internet service providers, the residences using those and all IP addresses of houses and offices that use those services. Keep all the info in one location. Add the details of the internet service they are using and their IP address in the individual profile database.'

'Check that all of the data matches with the user profile and the IP address data collected from the service provider. Any new connection should be approved by us and get it linked to their SSN.'

'How is law and order handling this?'

Arjun tries to connect the events in his mind. She presses nine, seven, and three. 9 might represent her entering the substation, while 7 could represent the gift in place. Three might be opening the breaker.

'Wait- wait. How will the other team members know she is prepared to pull the breaker? Or the other way around that.'

'Then nine may be the gift in place. Seven could be near the panel opened and prepared to pull the breaker. 3 could be pressed after the breaker has been opened.'

'Number 4 is still waiting.'

Arjun receives a call from the tech person explaining that the lights on both devices can be controlled by an outsider. By our understanding they could be operated by the unknown person. Could be the same guy missing at the malls. Also, could be the one who did that blast of the satellite equipment during the second attack.

The tech guy also attempts to synchronize the timelines.

'When the number 4 button is hit, green lights illuminate. Prior to then, yellow lights were blinking once the number 6 was touched which may indicate that the girls had entered the exhibition, sir.'

'Ok. Good.'

Arjun is now recreating the entire scene.

'Number ten is before the dead guy leaves the stalls. She enters the substation, hands them the present and presses the number nine. When he opens the back gate lock, he presses number eight.'

'Number 7 was completed by the lady at the panel door. For six, the girls entered the exhibition. This one was pressed by an outsider who most likely followed her from the stalls to the building.'

'After injecting the medication, push number five.'

'Number 4 comes from the operator, who is operating from a separate place, mostly on the college campus, because he needs to be within the device's range to communicate. May be a signal to proceed for the next step and also provide a bit of illumination in the room. Number three, she removes the breaker. The power is gone. Number two: they attack her and take her to the backstage area.'

'We stop there.'

Arjun is excited at last. He now knows the size of his opponent's team and how they are communicating.

Another inquiry comes up. How did they communicate during the second strike, when no such sequences were used? What about their exit points from college?

They discussed about communication. The next step is to track their location. He continues to watch footage of their escape points and visits them himself.

Seated in his car Arjun yet again appears to be puzzled and clueless.

Chapter - 11
The Three Colours

'Collect feedback from each and every officer what kind of problems they are facing? What is their current workload? Are there any methods implemented to bring predictive policing into practice.'

'We have to update all our code of conduct and procedurals conducted for investigation.'

'I'd like to see the health reports for everyone on that list. I want all of the cops to be in terrific shape. Once every three months, conduct physical and psychological tests? If extra training is required, provide it. Keep them updated.'

'Same like police stations I want to see all the courts' location on the map.'

'Gather data on the crime rate in each area. Segregate the areas based on the amount of money or capital involved as well as the population involved. It could be industrial or residential.'

'If you give me the location of both the stations and courts. I shall set the locations of new police stations and courts. Let us estimate their construction cost beforehand. I'll try to map it out with my planning.'

'This service will be offered solely by our company. There will be no more third parties. I'd want to see a list of existing member companies. Estimate their reactions. At the very least, we will do the recruiting part. Both parties can decide on operations.'

'Estimate the number of votes we will lose if we go full throttle.'

Colors continue to flash out while he sleeps. Red, green, and yellow continuously flash simultaneously the image of the car as well. He suddenly awakens. Tries to see the footage again. Couldn't find anything significant and falls asleep slowly.

He wakes up in the morning. He seemed disappointed. His thoughts constantly return to the subject of where the kidnappers are staying. How do they know that they're supposed to be there?

His team is yet to find a pattern from the exit points and the manner they escaped on each of the occasions.

He comes down to leave for college. His mother inquires as to why he appears to be disappointed.

'Are you thinking about your project? His mother takes him to the meditation room.'

'Everything will be taken care of. Don't worry my son. She adds up.'

The electricity goes off as he begins to close his eyes. The room turns dark and a small flickering lamp glows amidst the darkness. He looks at his mother.

She gives an optimistic look.

He closes his eyes once again. Flashes of power cuts in the exhibition come to his mind. The three lights start to glow in his mind along with the car.

He opens his eyes and looks at the flickering lamp down under.

He closes his eyes once again and opens them in a flash of delight.

He exits the room, collects his bag and quickly begins to leave the home.

His mother urges him to have breakfast. He claims to have some urgent work and will have breakfast at the college.

'We finished developing the organizational chart and the workflow. We know how long each stage will take to complete. Look for any changes that need to be made to speed up the process.'

'Find the problem statement.'

'Let me give an example. The delay could be lack of funds, lack of manpower, or excessive processing time. External interference, lack of infrastructure, working conditions, customer support, legal systems. Like this it could be related to anything.'

'Each of you is considered for this position because you work in a specific industry, department or ministry. Prepare those reports for your concerned department.'

'I want presentations from you. I will give schedule for presentations. Budgets should also be estimated. Your spokesperson and your lead have already received a copy of the budget allocations. Whatever solution you want us to consider, explain it so that it benefits both the parties. One is the company and the other one being the people that is you.'

'Don't limit your ideas to budgets allotted. We will collectively take a call on budget implementation. Just go full throttle on implementation of your ideas.'

'Your approach to planning and implementation should be simple and clear so that the general public and the Board of Directors could easily understand.'

Arjun drives his car to a location and stops there. He looks at a big hoarding, with an advertisement for the car. Three distinct colour schemes surround the hoarding. Red, yellow, and green. Red is currently highlighted.

He snaps a photo of the hoarding. He wakes up one of his teammates. Updates him on the situation. Orders to inquire about all of the areas where car hoardings are installed in the city.

Consider hoardings that are taller and located in residential areas. Consider these types of venues first.

After a while he gets the locations of all hoardings. He instructs his men to divide them into residential and non-residential regions. Arjun specifically pins down certain locations and urges them to inquire about anyone who is staying for rent or has rented a residence in the recent 5 months.

'Excellent work guys. Move to those places immediately.' Meanwhile, Arjun receives word that they have discovered three houses where hoardings are clearly visible and direct light is falling into their rooms.

'The bad news is that they left the house two days ago.'

'Also, one such board is near Meghna's house which is placed in such a way that it can be seen clearly from the girl's hostel and the sniper's location.'

He instructs the crew to gather as much information as possible. 'Are they employed anywhere. Any Id Proofs submitted. Who are the owners?'

'Work on it'...

Later on, he himself visits those places and appears to be disappointed again.

While everyone is preparing their problem statements, Arjun asks for the updated voter data from his secretary. Details about everyone who has registered and is eligible to vote.

'Divide them demographically, by profession (job or business), by department and by family tree if exists. In terms of both community and finances.'

'I need segregation of people on above lines and estimate how many votes we can expect. Meanwhile Arjun is working on his own set of recommendations.'

The day before the final project review.

Chapter - 12
The Final Run

The day before the final project review.

Arjun is preparing for his last presentation. Before leaving the house, his father calls him and wants to know about the exam result as it is reported in the newspaper. Arjun admits that he failed the exam.

His father chastises him that he is useless and should look at what other guys of his age are accomplishing.

'Do you have any shame?'

'You don't come with us to any gatherings. Never meet anyone. Does not talk to anyone including your parents.'

'I assumed you were preparing for the exam and working on the project. Complete waste of money and time I spent on you.'

'What will you do after PG? Are you looking for any work? Do you have answers to these questions? You are a completely useless individual.'

'You did well in your undergrad. What happened now?'

'All your friends have settled down successfully, and the most of them are getting married while you are stranded in life.'

'My life as well as yours. Stranded.'

'What is your identity other than being my son?'

'NO JOB. NO MARRIAGE. NO FAMILY.'

'NO LIFE at all.'

'Nobody should have a son like you.'

Arjun doesn't say anything and simply stands in front of his father.

His father gutted and frustrated tells him to leave for college.

Furious with his father words Arjun leaves the house and comes to college.

Meghna also has her semester exam starting tomorrow.

She goes to meet their guru along with the hall ticket to seek their blessing. It's also an auspicious day, the place is crowded.

Arjun starts to attend the meeting along with the other spokesperson. As per the schedule given by Arjun each department's meeting is conducted. The presentations are rolled on. Because everything is virtual, the team members found it difficult to adapt but gradually come to terms with the platform.

Arjun is pleased with the presentations because the majority of the proposals discussed are in line with his opinions or ideas.

He directs them to create a detailed budget implementation plan that specifies how much money goes to which department and is spent on which works.

He also instructs the spokespersons to become familiar with the data and proposals which are framing since they have a significant role in the subsequent stages.

Also prepare final proposals as early as possible.

Each team has to submit a brief proposal to the organizers which will be made public. Arjun asks the assistant how much time is still left for submission.

'Three weeks sir.'

After reaching the college he receives a message from his guide inquiring about the status of the project report. He barely pays attention. Keeps his phone in his bag.

Instead of heading to his department, he immediately heads to the ground. He goes to the change room takes off his tracker and walks to the ground in his shorts. Sets his things aside and prepares to go for a run.

One of Arjun's associates isn't feeling well; he attempts to contact Arjun to inform him of his unavailability. But couldn't reach him.

Arjun's starts sprinting fast in the ground - words said by his father keep running in his mind. His face turns red.

Meanwhile, Meghna is abducted after she completes her visit with the guru's. Vijay and his staff are short-staffed. The kidnappers escape in a flash.

She is on sedatives.

The final proposals are submitted by Arjun's team. The next stage begins in two weeks. They can relax for a while now.

Vijay and his team have been left behind once again. They also attempt to contact Arjun, who is still unavailable. Arjun is still sprinting in the ground.

The CEO now tries to contact Arjun. But the result remains the same.

A day after submission, news drops by- that internal poll will be conducted after 7 days of submission to know the public buzz. Arjun is looking forward to the day.

Arjun eventually stops sprinting and sits beneath the tree. Takes out the mobile from the bag and discovers a slew of missed calls.

He calls Vijay and learns about the situation. The kidnappers have made their vehicle unavailable to follow once more. The backup vehicle has just arrived but there is no update on the girl's current location.

Arjun assures him that he will find a solution. Meanwhile let me if there is an update.

The internal poll is conducted. While the poll results are to be announced shortly Arjun looks at the photo of Annanya beside his monitor.

Annanya is seen crying in her room. Having her back to the wall, sitting on the floor. She tells Arjun to leave from that place.

Arjun gets up from his chair and starts to move towards the bottle on the other end of the room. Takes the bottle from the fridge. He finally opens the bottle, takes a glass and fills it completely.

Back at home, Arjun's father appears heartbroken and tells his wife that he is unable to comprehend whether it is him using such harsh words or his sons silence that is making him feel the way he is feeling at that moment. Gutted.

Arjun comes back to his working desk with the glass in his hand. The counting has begun and the score of each team is going up and down on the monitor screen. He continues to look at the photo. He keeps the glass in between the monitor and the photo frame.

Seated under the tree he picks up his bag and starts sprinting towards the main entrance gate

The counting is done and the scores are frozen. Arjun's team finishes third. Arjun looks disappointed.

His father too looks very disappointed and unhappy.

While sprinting he takes his mobile to call someone.

Arjun approaches her. Kneels on the floor. Keeps one letter in her lap. Last one. He takes both her hands into his.

With the result he gets frustrated and leans forward to pick the glass.

The name on the caller Id shows "RUDRA".

She is still crying. You asked me what love meant for me right...

LOVE is...

www.ingramcontent.com/pod-product-compliance
Lightning Source LLC
LaVergne TN
LVHW061549070526
838199LV00077B/6967